OXFORD ORATIONS

*A selection of orations
by Godfrey Bond*

Public Orator 1980–1992

Godfrey Bond

OXFORD ORATIONS

A selection of orations by Godfrey Bond

Public Orator 1980–1992

Oxbow Books

Published by
Oxbow Books, Park End Place, Oxford

ISBN 1 84217 016 3

A CIP record of this book is available from the British Library

This book is available from

Oxbow Books, Park End Place, Oxford OX1 1HN
Tel: 01865-241249; Fax: 01865-794449
Email: oxbow@oxbowbooks.com

and

The David Brown Book Co.
PO Box 511, Oakville, CT 06779
Tel: (860) 945-9329; Fax: (860) 945-9468
Email: david.brown.bk.co@snet.net

and

from our website

www.oxbowbooks.com

Printed in Great Britain
at the Alden Press, Oxford

CONTENTS

GODFREY BOND AS PUBLIC ORATOR

THERE are two common misconceptions about the work of the Public Orator. One is that he composes the speeches in English and then translates them into Latin. The other is that he has a team of researchers who present him with the facts of the honorand's life and work. Neither was true of Godfrey's work. He would walk around Boar's Hill with his Rhodesian Ridgeback, Mungo, turning over phrases in his mind. An envelope, an old bill, was seized to write down a choice sentence. Much would be rejected as he worked to give the speech balance. I used to protest if he gave too much prominence to the domestic details of his women honorands. We sometimes argued fiercely over the English translations – and he didn't always win.

If he were asked if he disliked someone he wrote about, he quoted a description given to him in a newspaper on his appointment – 'a hired mouth'. Inevitably the character and achievements of some honorands appealed less than others, and the slyest of digs might creep in, unspotted by anyone except those who knew his style very well. He wished always to write in clear simple Latin so that it could be understood by those who had a minimal knowledge of the language – he resisted the complicated or the showy. He enjoyed greatly switching to Lucretian verse to expound scientific theories which had been explained to him by helpful colleagues. He spent the Easter vacation receiving 'tutorials' from friends or from those who knew the work of the honorands, reading their works or listening to their music. This expansion of knowledge was, for him, one of the most stimulating aspects of being a Public Orator.

It was rare for an honorand to acknowledge his endeavours or to thank him for his work, though he was delighted to be kissed by Kiri Te Kanawa. Three presents gave him pleasure – a silver spoon with the Zimbabwe emblem from the Rhodes Trustees; a silver spoon engraved with the Imperial chrysanthemum from Prince Naruhito of Japan, and a book on Romanesque architecture from King Baudouin. Most honorands stood beside him in the Sheldonian looking confident and distinguished, but there were some touching exceptions. Dorothy Hodgkin looked like a little old lady out with her shopping bag. Peter Pears was so frail that he couldn't climb the steps to receive his scroll and Harold Macmillan, the Chancellor, was too unsteady to go down to meet him; the Senior Proctor acted as runner between the two. Andrei Sakharov, after Godfrey had finished his oration, turned and shook him by the hand. Jacqueline du Pré was in her wheelchair; the oration about her was one of the most difficult he ever had to write. Eva Turner the singer, then aged ninety-two, turned to acknowledge the applause and waved with all the grace of an operatic diva, whereupon the applause doubled in volume.

He was proud of being an Irishman and often used this fact to give extra warmth to a speech. He regretted greatly that Oxford was slower than Cambridge in offering an Honorary Degree to Mary Robinson, President of Ireland, so that he missed the opportunity to present her himself. It would have pleased Godfrey that from his oration for Garret FitzGerald (the then Taioseach), the present Dublin University Orator picked out the subtleties of his reference to the citizens of Dublin who called their leader "Garret the Good", while the Lord Chief Justice of Northern Ireland, his former pupil, exulted in Godfrey's Latin for 'Ulster says No'. Garret FitzGerald was one of twelve honorands nominated by Lord Jenkins on his appointment as Chancellor of Oxford University (an ancient privilege). Two other major occasions in Oxford necessitated additional orations – the eightieth anniversary of the Rhodes scholarships and the hundred and fiftieth annual meeting of the British Association for the Advancement of Science.

In 1987, an *annus mirabilis*, Godfrey wrote twenty-three speeches ranging from the Librarian of the Hope entomological collection to the King of Belgium. He presented six members of the Royal Houses of Europe and Japan which enabled him to quote with glee a remark of Provost Mahaffy of Trinity College Dublin (his own University), 'He was the nicest King I knew'. The orations for MAs given often to those who served Oxford University for many years whether as Marshal, or chief technician in the Nuffield Department of Anaesthetics, or instrument maker in the Department of Geology (to name but a few), gave him more time to expand on the activities of the honorands and to use a more playful style. The orations for Encaenia had of necessity to be somewhat shorter as there could be as many as eight people presented together. One of these might be a Head of State or a King or Queen receiving a Degree by Diploma, and he had to use a traditional legalistic form. This could be countered by informality: Prince Charles rang Godfrey the night before his presentation to ask him the Latin for 'humble fenman' – though the Prince quickly returned to English in his reply, to the relief of the Sheldonian audience.

Godfrey's voice was strong, and he never needed a microphone. I would sit where he could see me and make a signal if he were galloping along too quickly. As always, clarity and simplicity were his aims. He enjoyed the challenge of encapsulating a life, of picking out small details – it was not his wish to give a résumé from *Who's Who*. In his twelve years, 1980–92, as Orator he composed one hundred and thirty-nine orations, so that it has been a difficult task to reduce the number for this volume. In this I have been greatly helped by two of his closest friends and colleagues – Donald Russell of St John's College and Margaret Howatson of St Anne's College, who did the proof reading. I hope that the publication of these speeches may give others the pleasure they gave him.

Alison Bond

GODFREY WILLIAM BOND 1925–1997

Memorial address by Sir Robert Carswell
Lord Chief Justice of Northern Ireland

GODFREY BOND represented for me many of the things that I liked and admired about the Oxford which I knew as an undergraduate – the personal interest of a tutor in the progress and welfare of his pupils, the standards of scholarship and intellectual integrity preserved and passed on to successive generations and the forging of friendships which endured long beyond student days. If these have declined in Oxford in general in recent years under the compulsion of other pressures, it would be a loss, and I hope that they have not.

To know the man you must know his origins. Godfrey was brought up in Belfast, where his father was a civil servant, and his Ulster roots ran deep. But he also had a long Southern connection through his mother Janet Godfrey, descended from the Digges LaTouche family, Anglo-Irish who played a considerable role in earlier Irish affairs, and through that connection as well as that of Alison he always had an affinity with and an affection for Dublin.

He received his school education in Belfast. He was hardly your typical schoolboy hero: tall, a little awkward, not unlike a juvenile version of Monsieur Hulot, intellectually precocious and seriously lacking in the sort of co-ordination which is required for excellence in ball games, he did not fit the pattern of every school. But when he became a pupil of The Royal Belfast Academical Institution he found the stimulus of high-quality teaching and the tolerant atmosphere which enabled him to blossom, and he retained always a great affection for Inst.

After two years code-breaking in Bletchley Godfrey entered Trinity College, Dublin, where he had strong family links, through his uncle Frank Godfrey, the Senior Tutor, and his aunt Chris, who was in charge of all the woman undergraduates. He had a brilliant university career. He became a Scholar of the House in his first year, a rare achievement, since it was won in open competition with undergraduates of all years. He crowned his Trinity career by obtaining high marks in his final classical examinations, winning a Gold Medal (then distinguished by the title of Large Gold Medal). Not content with that, he climbed the Trinity student's academic Everest by taking within a fortnight after his classical finals a second final examination, this time in Mental and Moral Sciences.

In 1950, after a brief spell at St John's, Godfrey was elected a Fellow of Pembroke, where he took up his life's work. He was a Fellow of the College for all of 42 years, a record which it would be hard to match in modern times. Pembroke was then a very different place from that which it later became. Both the student body and the governing body were very much smaller. It was a happy college, but it was as well that the much-maligned Norrington tables were not then in existence, because Pembroke would certainly have been bumping along the bottom.

Godfrey set out to change that in his own subject. He harnessed youthful energy to his ambition to make Pembroke a college which counted in classical studies, and over the next few years he succeeded nobly in achieving his aim. He wanted to attract promising entrants, and he knew that to do so Pembroke had to have a reputation for producing good academic results. Godfrey made a huge commitment in time, effort and nervous energy to accomplish the osmotic transfer of learning to his early intakes of pupils, a commitment which would, I think, be inconceivable today. Those who studied in the early days under Godfrey Bond can testify to having received personal tuition of a quality and intensity which few universities in the world can ever have provided for their students. As one of the beneficiaries of this effort, I know very well the enormous advantage that it afforded me in facing the rigorous test of classical knowledge and skills – not to mention mental and also physical stamina – that Honour Moderations then presented. It was not exclusively his prize pupils, however, who benefited from Godfrey's efforts. 'Added value' may be one of the pieces of current educational jargon, but Godfrey knew very well its implications, for he encouraged and brought on students of a whole range of abilities to produce their best.

Tutorials with Godfrey were not for the dilettante undergraduate who had only a passing acquaintance with the work that he was supposed to prepare. Godfrey made it very clear what he wished you to turn out for him. One was expected to present one's prose and verse compositions at a set time in advance of the tutorial, to allow Godfrey time to peruse and correct them, and the valuable teaching time was used in dissection and instruction, broadening into literary discussion. If one's offering was not up to standard, Godfrey would, as we used to say, humph at you, and give what we called the Godfrey stare – not like Socrates, glowering like a bull, but slightly sidelong over the glasses, skellying as his Ulster forebears would say, and fastening very firmly upon one's deficiencies.

That academic precision and intellectual rigour, combined with literary perception and sensibility, instilled into Godfrey's pupils an appreciation of the need for intellectual discipline, a passion for accuracy and a craftsmanlike facility with language which have been a glorious benison for so many of us. It was that teaching which struck a spark and ignited the tinder of our minds at a time when it could accomplish most and started us on a path that we could not have found without his guidance.

If this picture of Godfrey Bond at work were to give the impression of a narrow pedant or one who was only interested in the intellectual force-feeding of his students, it would be utterly misleading. He was a man of wide and varied tastes who pursued and cared for the literary as well as the necessary linguistic aspects of his area of study. He produced two commentaries on plays of Euripides which are a permanent addition to classical scholarship, the fragmentary *Hypsipyle* (whose decrypting no doubt owed something to his Bletchley training) and the *Heracles*. Equally important, he concerned himself with the welfare of the undergraduates in Pembroke, first with his own pupils and then more widely during his long periods of office as Dean. No account of Godfrey's college life would be complete without a description of his decanal lunches; I must myself pass that up, as they did not commence until after my time, but they became a celebrated part of Pembroke life.

Godfrey filled many of the offices in his college, and made a significant contribution to the life of the University. He served as Senior Proctor, he sat on the general Board of the Faculties, and then was elected in 1980 to the office by which he was best known and from which he derived great pleasure, that of University Orator. He presented a succession of distinguished honorary graduands for degrees, in orations phrased in elegant and felicitous Latin and laced with a puckish wit, which were based upon meticulous research into the careers and merits of those whom he presented.

Those who have written of Godfrey Bond since his death have referred to his Latin rendering of Cardinal Hume's hot line to his priests or his splendid phrase for jumbo jets, *balaenae ballistariae* – 'catapulted whales'. He took electron microscopes in his stride, and was rather proud of his ingenious translation of DNA, which might defeat many scholars. My personal favourite, however, was his presentation of Dr Garret Fitzgerald, former Taoiseach of Ireland, in 1987, when after referring to the Anglo-Irish Agreement he tucked in the sly phrase, *in regione boreali multi adhuc adversantur* – 'Ulster says No'.

This was the public face of Godfrey Bond, the product of the university platform by which he became well known far beyond his own college. But I incline to the view that if he had been asked at the time of his retirement what he thought most worth while in his career he would have plumped for his work in Pembroke, sparking off thoughts in young minds, showing them the importance of achieving the right mixture of inspiration and perspiration in matters intellectual, guiding them with wisdom and encouragement, and demonstrating that those rather older than themselves can like and befriend the young in a way which brings the generations together. This is his *monumentum aere perennius*.

I have left the most important thing to the last. I can almost hear a spectral reminder from Godfrey, but I am not about to neglect the essential. His wife and family were not just a central part of Godfrey's adult life, they gave it meaning and substance. In 1959 he married Alison, daughter of Mr Justice Kingsmill Moore, a distinguished member of the Irish Supreme Court and Visitor of Trinity College, Dublin. He and Godfrey took much pleasure in each other's company and in KM's visits to Boar's Hill and Pembroke. Alison and their children Catherine, Elwyn and Kingsmill formed a true family with Godfrey which was a centre and a base and a refuge for him. Together they made their house at Boar's Hill a truly hospitable place to visit. It was a great joy to Godfrey that his family was increased by two grandchildren, the younger born just before his death.

How sad it was that Godfrey was robbed by illness of his retirement time, from which he could have derived so much pleasure and in which he would have pursued his study of Euripides, to the great benefit of the world of classical studies. He died at the relatively early age of 71, with much yet to do. But we who remain can now think of the many things which he did achieve and the many ways in which he left this world a better place. Let us thank God for the life of Godfrey William Bond and think of him in the words of Jacob Rudin:

> When we are dead, and people weep for us and grieve, let it be because we touched their lives with beauty and simplicity. Let it not be said that life was good to us: but, rather, that we were good to life.

THE ORATIONS

EDVARDVS ABRAHAM

VIR sequitur qui heros inter heroas versatus est, salutatione heroica dignissimus:

> e tenebris tantis tam clarum extollere lumen
> qui primus potuisti.

laudem enim Oxonienses maximam in hoc saeculo ideo cepimus quod *penicillini* usu hic invento terror morbis plurimis ereptus est. perspicite, quaeso, titulos inter rosas iuxta pontem nostrum antiquum incisos decemvirorum qui inter belli maximi minas victoriam hanc gentibus omnibus communem reportaverunt. nomina quaedam Oxoniensibus bene nota invenietis: FLOREY, CHAIN, HEATLEY, SANDERS, ABRAHAM. penicillini autem quae essent elementa primus hic adiuvante Ernesto Boris Chain collegisque aliis doctissimis demonstravit; qua re συνθέσει ut vocatur, subtili fungorum culturae coniuncta penicillinum creare et pervulgare licuit.

Erant tamen homines quibus remedia haec nova nocebant, erant morbi qui pellaciis penicillini non capiebantur; imminebat etiam istud – sive fermentum sive monstrum taetrum vocari debet – *beta* lactamasium quod penicillino medenti officiebat. inventione nempe altera opus erat. ecce qui inventor subvenit, qui fungis in Sardinia primo repertis subtilius decoctis *cephalosporinorum* usum invenit atque elementa eorum septem cum Guio Newton indagavit, quorum unum praecipue, cephalosporinum quoddam littera 'C' notatum, *beta* illud noxium valebat vincere: littera vere litterae contraria. cui inventioni nonne notam illam praestantissimam *alpha* oportet adsignari?

Victoria autem hac parta optime usus est. res enim tanta sollertia gessit ut cephalosporinis per orbem terrarum venditis pars sua pretiorum fiduciariis quibusdam doctis redderetur, quibus adiumenta plurima debemus academici. nam auri grande pondus cum duorum Professorum gravitate adaequatum Universitati pensaverunt, biophysicos adiuverunt ut officinam super domum fermentorum aedificent; scientiarum etiam officinis machinas, Collegiis collegas – prospere experto mihi credite – dederunt.

Praesento vobis Eduardum Abraham, Equitem auratum, Excellentissimi Ordinis Imperii Britannici Commendatorem, Societatis Regiae Sodalem, Collegiorum septem honoris causa Socium, Professorem iam emeritum, ut admittatur honoris causa ad gradum Doctoris in Scientia.

SIR EDWARD ABRAHAM
Discoverer of the structure of penicillin

S IR Edward Abraham deserves a hero's salute as a member of a heroic team of scientists:

> Hail to the man who showed a path for men,
> Lightening our darkness.

This generation of Oxford men and women has won great praise from the discovery here at Oxford of the clinical uses of penicillin, which has taken the terror out of many diseases. The names of ten individuals who amid the menaces of war won this victory for the common benefit of all nations may be found inscribed on stone in the rose garden at Magdalen Bridge. Among them certain names well known to us in Oxford stand out: FLOREY, CHAIN, HEATLEY, SANDERS, ABRAHAM. Our honorand Edward Abraham was the first man to work out the molecular structure of penicillin, a discovery he made in collaboration with Ernst Boris Chain and other colleagues, which led to the manufacture and distribution of semi-synthetic penicillins.

But there were still patients who were sensitive to penicillin and infections which were resistant to its blandishments; and we were threatened by a troublesome pest, the enzyme *beta-lactamase*, which inhibited the healing effect of penicillin. So a new discovery was needed; and here is the man who came to our aid and made it. He discovered the efficacy of *cephalosporins,* which are derived from a subtle brew of a fungus found originally in Sardinia. With the help of Guy Newton he worked out the seven different elements of the cephalosporin mould, one of which, the famous cephalosporin 'C', was able to counteract the noxious *beta*-lactamase: here indeed is a violent clash of letters. We may properly call this a discovery of *alpha* quality.

Having won this victory he followed it up effectively. He contrived that his share of the profits from the world-wide sale of cephalosporin should accrue to a body of academic Trustees. From them we in Oxford have derived many advantages. They have given the University a substantial funding sufficient to carry the weight of two new Professorships, and have enabled the molecular biophysicists to build a place for their work on top of the Enzyme Laboratory. They have provided departments with apparatus and colleges with colleagues – believe me, for my own college has greatly benefited from the Abraham Trust.

I present Sir Edward Abraham, CBE, FRS, Honorary Fellow of seven colleges, The Queen's College, Lincoln College, Lady Margaret Hall, St Peter's, Linacre, Wolfson and Green Colleges, Professor Emeritus, for admission to the Honorary Degree of Doctor of Science.

1984

DAVID FREDERICVS ATTENBOROUGH

ADEST vir in rebus plurimis versatus, quem gorillas ingentes (simias dico, non feminas istas incultas) salutatione amicissima foventes inTViti estis. quod qui semel spectarit pro certo habebit vere hunc in praelectione nuper pronuntiavisse, in eius modi concordia positam esse felicitatem.

Zoologiam quondam geologiamque apud Cantabrigienses didicit, anthropologiam apud Londinienses. πολυμαθέστατος iam dudum factus est qui in loca maxime remota itinera tot tantaque fecerit ut animalia rarissima excipiat quae ad vivaria nostra adportet. non difficile esse scripsit animal aliquod ignotum invenire. invenit ipse fortasse *cynocephalum* illum fabulosum; indrim certe summo labore indagatum phototypice depinxit, lemures insula Hannonis avectos Londinium reportavit. dubito vero utrum Ulixi eum comparem an Plinio, librorum triginta septem historiae naturalis scriptori; quippe qui illo doctior esse videatur, hoc sane facetior.

In animo enim habet populo nostro talia domi spectanti doctrinam pariter et delectationem praebere. Nam bene cognovit verba quaedam Horati quae paulum mutata repetam:

> omne tulit punctum qui miscuit utile dulci,
> *spectantes* delectando pariterque monendo.

Neque animalia solum exquisivit, sed flores, personas caelatas, atque adeo homines indagavit:

> πολλῶν δ' ἀνθρώπων ἴδεν ἄστεα καὶ νόον ἔγνω.

Pygmaeos visit nec non homines solitarios qui Burolulam incolunt, Tongae ritum sollemnem Kavae spectavit, gazam regiam Montezumae, Obae caelaturas aeneas nobis exhibuit.

Ars huic res hominesque explorandi laboribus res administrandi diu quondam cessit. Societati enim Britannicae imagines vocesque per aethera iaculandi causa institutae adscriptus annos octo disposuit atque ordinavit vel multa vel omnia quae nostri intuebantur. postea tandem ad imagines faciendas reversus de animalium generibus rursus inquisivit quo quodque genus in rerum natura munere fungeretur. nuper etiam maris Mediterranei regionumque adfinium studia fecit, paradisi illius antiquissimi, Aegyptorum Cretum Graecorum Romanorum nutricis. hoc duce animalia sacra antiquorum spectavimus, castella quoque ab eis qui itinera sacra sub cruce fecerunt aedificata; ab hoc de silvis maximis succisis, de leonibus Graecis, de triumphis infidelium audivimus. quae invenerant geologi oecologi archaeologi rerum gestarum scriptores sollertissime semper adhibuit, doctissime conglutinavit, picturis splendidis illustravit.

Praesento vobis virum qui plurimorum animos historiae naturalis amore atque adeo humanitatis studio incendit, Davidem Fredericum Attenborough, Equitem Auratum, Excellentissimi Ordinis Imperii Britannici Commendatorem, Societatis Regiae Sodalem, Collegii de Clare apud Cantabrigienses honoris causa Socium, ut admittatur honoris causa ad gradum Doctoris in Scientia.

DAVID ATTENBOROUGH
Zoologist

HERE is a man of vast experience, whom you have seen on your television screens receiving an affectionate welcome from a troop of full-sized gorillas. Anyone who has witnessed this will appreciate the conclusion of his Baggs Memorial Lecture that harmony of this kind must underlie all true happiness.

Sir David Attenborough read Zoology and Geology at Cambridge and studied Anthropology at London University. What first turned him into a polymath was his *Zoo Quest* programme, which sent him off exploring little-known parts of the world to find rare animals for our zoological collections. 'It is not difficult to discover an unknown animal,' he writes. He himself may well have discovered the legendary *cynocephalus;* at any rate after a long search he tracked down an indris and photographed it, and he has brought lemurs back from Madagascar to Regent's Park. I am not sure whether to compare him to Ulysses or Pliny, the author of thirty-seven books of *Natural History*. While he is more scholarly than the former, he is certainly more witty than the latter.

The purpose of his programmes is to provide both instruction and entertainment for the public. He is well aware of the truth of Horace's dictum, which needs only one small alteration:

> Top ratings go to the man who mixes fun and instruction,
> With simultaneous effect delighting and teaching the *viewers*.

Our honorand was not content to search out animals. His interest has extended to flowers, masks and men.

> Many cities of men he saw, and learned
> the mind of their peoples.

He has visited the pygmies and the hermits of Booroloola; in Tonga he has been present at the rites of Kava; he has shown us the treasure of Montezuma and the bronzes of the Oba. For some time his skill at investigating men and things took second place to administrative work. For eight years he was in charge of our viewing, first as Controller of BBC2 and then as Director of Television Programmes for the BBC. After that he returned to making programmes. In *Life on Earth* he studied the part played by each group of animals in the whole history of nature. More recently in *The First Eden* he has investigated the lands of the Mediterranean which once nurtured the Egyptians, Cretans, Greeks and Romans. With him as our guide we have seen the sacred animals of former peoples and the castles of the Crusaders. We have learned of the destruction of vast forests, of lions in Greece, of the victories of Islam. He has shown the greatest skill and learning in combining the discoveries of geologists, ecologists, archaeologists and historians with splendid photography.

I present a man who has inspired a great many people with a love for natural history and also with a zeal for humane studies, Sir David Attenborough, CBE, FRS, Honorary Fellow of Clare College, Cambridge, for the Honorary Degree of Doctor of Science.

1988

ALFREDVS BRENDEL

IN Austria hic educatus est, terra maximis auctoribus musicis divite, quibus ipse operam maximam dedit. fidem autem eam modulatur qua nervi permulti malleolis propriis pulsantur, a contionibus frequentissimis per omnes quot sunt continentes auditus est. qui docente Eduino Fischer multa se didicisse adfirmat, doctrinae tamen musicae pleraque a Musa ipsa tradita accepit, qui potest idem atque vates ille epicus sibi vindicare:

> αὐτοδίδακτος δ᾽ εἰμί, θεὸς δέ μοι ἐν φρεσὶν οἴμας
> παντοίας ἐνέφυσεν.

Audaciam autem habet cum summa doctrina consociatam. nam opera omnia quae fidi isti aptaverat Ludovicus maximus discis ceratis edidit, itaque opera quaedam minime nota pervulgavit. de labore hoc ingenti, quem ante annum tricesimum quintum complevit, audite quid ipse scripserit. *'aliquid . . . invadere magnum* mens agitabat, in laborem me ingurgitavi.' eodem fere modo opera Mozarti Schubertique memoriae tradidit.

Fidicines praecipue illos aversatur qui artificia adhibeant, praestigiis etiam delectationis causa utantur. auctoribus autem ipse plurimis laetatur, illos tamen mavult qui inter classicos recte numerati sunt, quorum scripta summa accuratione interpretatur. clarissime enim docet eadem eos ratione diminutionis uti solere quae picturis insit, qua proxima lineis maioribus, ultima minoribus depicta sint. novistis fortasse id quod de Schuberti Ludovicique istius arte scripsit, oblectamenti tamen causa repeto, *ratione architectonica hunc uti, illum somnambulatoria.*

At difficillimum est voce pedestri ingenium huius musicum exponere. testis est praestantior vocandus qui et lingua et scriptis est cum Ludovico ipso coniunctus, cuius versibus paulo maiora canamus:

> legibus inservire decet cui magna paranda;
> limitibus certis instantibus eminet orbi
> magnum opus artificis magni: modo lege sub ipsa
> libertatem adfert aliquando optantibus aetas.

Praesento vobis Alfredum Brendel, virum μουσικώτατον, ut admittatur honoris causa ad gradum Doctoris in Musica.

ALFRED BRENDEL
Musician

ALFRED BRENDEL was brought up in Austria, a land rich in great musical composers, to whom he has devoted much of his life. He has played the piano at concerts in every continent in the world. He is indebted, he says, to the teaching of Edwin Fischer, but most of his knowledge of music comes from the Muse herself; he can make the same claim as the Homeric bard:

> Self-taught I am, the god implanted strains
> Of all kinds in my mind.

He has a combination of boldness and great learning. He made a recording of all the piano works of Beethoven and thereby gave prominence to a number of little-known pieces. What has he written about this considerable task, which he finished before the age of thirty-five? 'I just plunged into an adventure.' In much the same way he has recorded the piano works of Mozart and Schubert.

He is especially opposed to pianists who use artificial devices and even tricks to please their audience. He himself enjoys a great many composers, but prefers those who are properly termed 'classical'. He interprets their music with rigorous accuracy. His exposition of their use of 'foreshortening' is particularly clear. You perhaps know his enjoyable *dictum* that 'Beethoven composes like an architect, Schubert like a sleepwalker'.

But it is far too difficult to expound Alfred Brendel's musical ability in the prose of an address. We must summon a witness from a higher plane to assist us, one who is linked with Beethoven himself by his language and his writings: the poetry of Goethe may serve to heighten the tone:

> Wer Großes will, muß sich zusammenraffen;
> In der Beschränkung zeigt sich erst der Meister,
> Und das Gesetz nur kann uns Freiheit geben.

I present Alfred Brendel, a man who radiates music, for admission to the Honorary Degree of Doctor of Music.

1983

SYDNEY BRENNER

A ENIGMATE genitivo soluto moleculisque vitalibus iam bene cognitis maximo fervore aestuabant studia biologorum, quorum pars magna fuit vir quem nunc produco. nomen eius cum molecula quadam coniunctum est *nuntia* vocata, quae et mobilitate et claritate viget, quae propriae sunt nuntiorum virtutes.

Acidum hoc est *ribonuclearium* vocatum quod cellulae e parte interiore ad exteriora summa mobilitate fertur mandata certa reportans, πρωτεῖα ut rite creentur et formentur. de molecula hac multa indagando invenit: inesse triadas quasdam nucleotidorum ordine certo in catena dispositas – eae *coda* nominatae sunt – easdem quae in nucleo ipso subessent. hanc si intuearis, Illustrissime, quae tam vitalis et operosa est, iuste possis dicere, 'numen inest'. et recte quidem 'nuntia' vocata est. nonne Christiani isti pristini eos qui inter Deum gentemque humanam intercessores vadunt 'nuntios' vel ἀγγέλους appellabant?

Neque haec inferiora vitae elementa tantum scrutatus est: de nematodibus etiam, vermiculorum genere, permulta indagavit qualibus cellularum mutationibus alantur, moveantur, procreentur. de genere hoc vitae quod humilius imperitis forsitan esse videatur, utilia tamen plurima inventa sunt. etenim schola iam est, φροντιστήριον paene dixeram, virum doctorum qui vestigia huius secuti studia de vermiculis eisdem exercent.

Abundat ipse et mobilitate mentis et claritate, qui et iuvenibus studiosis et viris doctissimis libenter scientiam suam profert. κόσμου πολίτης est qui originem ducit ab Europae partibus ad orientem sitis, in Africa ulteriore educatus est, Oxoniam quondam advenit ut studia in officina Cyrilli Hinshelwood exerceret; cuius praeceptis doctus verbis maxima cum diligentia solet uti. nonne eos castigat qui sermone remissiore de clonum *bibliothecis* loquuntur, qui *acervis* potius sine ordine accumulati sunt?

Pronuntiat se delectationem e machinando maxime consequi, oblectamento valde Slavonico. decet ergo eum tamquam πολύμητιν salutare heroique isti omnium machinatorum maximo simillimum:

en alius fauste cursum complevit Ulixes.

Praesento vobis Sydney Brenner, Societatis Regiae Sodalem, Collegii Exoniensis honoris causa Socium, officinae moleculas vitales indagantium apud Cantabrigienses Praefectum, ut admittatur honoris causa ad gradum Doctoris in Scientia.

SYDNEY BRENNER
Molecular Biologist

DR Sydney Brenner's work is part – and a substantial part – of the big biological explosion which involved the solving of the genetic code and the establishment of the molecular basis of life. His name is especially associated with a molecule which has been given the name 'messenger', since it possesses the essential features of a messenger, mobility and clarity.

This molecule, messenger RNA, is a chemical substance which is dynamic, moving from the nucleus of a cell to its outer parts, bringing a message which activates and directs the formation of protein within the cell. In his extensive research on this molecule Dr Brenner established that it contains a chain of triplets, or sequences of nucleotides, which are the same as the triplets in the DNA of the nucleus; these have been termed 'codons'. If you contemplate this active and motivated substance, Sir, you inevitably have a strong feeling of supernatural power. And it is rightly named 'messenger'. Did not the early Christians call the intermediaries between God and man 'messengers' or ἄγγελοι, 'angels'?

At a higher level of life he has developed a whole school – Aristophanes would have called it a 'think-tank'– of scientists investigating the cell biology of a simple nervous system by working on worms, 'nematodes', a lowly form of life strangers to this discipline may think, but one which has yielded rich discoveries.

He himself is (like messenger RNA) both intellectually active and informative, glad to put his experience at the disposal of young scientists as well as his colleagues in molecular biology. He is a true cosmopolitan, for he can trace his origins to Eastern Europe, he was educated in South Africa, and he came years ago to Oxford to work with Sir Cyril Hinshelwood, to whom he owes his meticulous care in the use of words, objecting for instance to the jargon in 'libraries' of clones, which implies proper ordering, whereas clones really lie around in 'heaps'.

He announces publicly that his recreation is 'scheming', a truly Slavonic pastime. So we salute him as πολύητις, the epithet of Ulysses, greatest of schemers:

> Heureux qui comme Ulysse a fait un beau voyage.

I present Sydney Brenner, FRS, Honorary Fellow of Exeter College, Director of the Medical Research Council Laboratory of Molecular Biology at Cambridge University, for admission to the Honorary Degree of Doctor of Science.

1985

JOSEPHVS BRODSKY

POETAM produco, in urbe *Petro* natum. nam nomen antiquum adhibui quo utuntur incolae urbis amantissimi, uti scripsit ipse, quamvis hodie aliter vulgo appelletur.

Carminibus huius inest mirifica vis verborum, quae sensu amplissimo abundant, accuratissime exquisita, usum auctorum veterum saepe imitata, φωνάεντα συνετοῖσι. ecce 'πῦρ Προμηθέως' quod potissimum tamquam sacrum colendum esse censet. nonne *illi robur et aes triplex / circum pectus* sit, si quis non commoveatur elegis maximis in commemorationem Iohannis Donne conscriptis, vel versibus illis quos scripsit de sepulchris Iudaeorum in urbe sua mortuorum, de ecclesia ibidem Graecorum Odei causa aedificandi eversa? neque desunt artificia poetica; metrorum subest callida et docta variatio. de poetis autem aliis libellos ingenio cum erudito tum perspicaci scriptos edidit, Marina scilicet Tsvetaeva, Iosepho Mandelstam, Anna Akhmatova, quam maxime veneratur. opera etiam peregrinorum bene cognovit, ut qui libellos de carminibus Eugenii Montalis, Dereci Walcott scripserit. quid? carmen a Wystan nostro sub initio belli saevissimi compositum doctissime excussit atque enarravit.

Iniquissima igitur fortuna huic accidit ut poeta vitam degeret sub dominatione potentium qui carmen quodvis ab hoc amicisve scriptum pro *contumacia loquaci,* ut scripsit hic, haberent, eo tempore cum carmina clam edere, clam divulgare providentiae erat.

Anno autem aetatis vicesimo quinto ideo accusatus est quod poeta solum esset neque aliud haberet unde viveret. Cuius criminis damnatus in ergastulum remotum missus labores indignissimos diu pertulit. patria deinde expulsus est. o di immortales! nonne poena eius modi tam saeva est ut exsecranda omnibus esse videatur? itaque bona cum venia vestra, officio meo laudandi paulisper remisso, iudicium illud, iudicem istam *Savelyevam,* cui ipse in carmine quodam male dixit, auctoritate mea et totius Musarum collegii castigo respuo repudio.

Exsul iam diu litterarum scientiam Americanis impertitur, Collegio Montis ab ilice sacra nominati Professor adscitus. carmina libellique linguas iam in plurimas versi per orbem totum terrarum leguntur; libertate nuper apud Russos illucescente etiam in patria iam laudantur.

Praesento vobis poetam consummatum, poetarum Russicorum huius aetatis eminentissimum, praemio Nobeliano honoratum, laurea Musarum transatlanticarum nuperrime coronatum, Iosephum Brodsky, ut admittatur honoris causa ad gradum Doctoris in Litteris.

JOSEPH BRODSKY
Poet

I now present a poet, born at *Peter,* to give the city its old name, still used affectionately by the inhabitants of Petrograd, although there is another name in common use.

His poetry is marked by his intensely vivid use of language. The words he employs are carefully chosen and deeply significant, with echoes of former poetry, *speaking out to the knowledgeable.* Here is the *flame of Prometheus,* the teaching of which he regards as an over-riding and sacred objective. *Dull would he be of soul who could pass by* without being moved by Brodsky's great elegy for John Donne, or his verses on the Jewish Cemetery in his home city, or on the demolition of the Greek Church there to make way for a concert hall. His work is rich in poetic technique; underlying it there is a skilful and varied use of metre. He has published learned and penetrating essays on other poets, such as Marina Tsvetaeva, Osip Mandelstam, and Anna Akhmatova, whom he particularly reveres. He is also well read in foreign poets, having written essays on the poetry of Montale and Derek Walcott. He has indeed published a careful and detailed analysis and explanation of Auden's poem 'September 1, 1939'.

It was our honorand's particular ill-fortune to live his life as a poet under the tyranny of masters who regarded any poem by him or his friends as 'linguistic disobedience', as he terms it, and at a time when a prudent poet published and circulated his work in secret, using *samizdat.*

At the age of twenty-four he was arrested and tried on a charge of simply being a poet and having no other trade to sustain him. He was convicted and sent to a remote labour camp where he endured months of hard labour. He was then sent into exile. Great God! Such a savage punishment surely merits universal condemnation and horror. With your permission I will briefly set aside my duty of praising: by virtue of my authority and that of the whole body of the Muses I castigate this judgment and the judge *Savelyeva,* whom Brodsky execrates in one of his later poems.

He has now lived in exile for a long time, teaching literature in the United States as Professor at Mount Holyoke College. His poems and essays now circulate round the world, translated into many languages. Now that there is a new dawn of freedom in Russia, he is quoted even in his own country.

I present Joseph Brodsky, a poet of poets, a Nobel Prizeman and Poet Laureate-elect of the United States, the most eminent of modern Russian poets, for the Honorary Degree of Doctor of Letters.

1991

PRINCEPS AVGVSTISSIMVS IOHANNES CAROLVS HISPANIAE REX

CANCELLARIVS MAGISTRI SCHOLARES
VNIVERSITATIS OXONIENSIS
OMNIBVS AD QVOS PRAESENTES
LITTERAE PERVENERINT
SALVTEM IN DOMINO SEMPITERNAM

CVM diu ex more nobis fuerit illustrissimos Reges et Principes qui propter mores spectatos et fortia facta inclaruerint, eosque praesertim qui cum Regia nostra Domo adfinitate coniuncti sint, praecipuo aliquo honore quantum possumus ornare:

CVMQVE Princeps augustissimus Iohannes Carolus, Hispaniae Rex, Alphonsi illius praeclarissimi nepos a quo studia nostra Hispaniensia olim corroborata sunt (nonne studiorum eorundem Professor Oxoniensis Alphonsi cognomine gaudet?) Rex creatus summa vigilantia laboraverit ut partes valde diversas in concordiam adducat:

CVMQUE in Congregatione nostra nemo fere adsit quin coniurationis contra rem publicam Hispanorum abhinc annos quinque factae memor sit, noctisque praecipue illius notissimae qua silentibus inter arma legibus, curia militum copiis obsessa, rem publicam Rex solus salvam praestitit, provinciarum praefectis statim ut milites in castris cohiberent praemonitis atque imagine sua per aethera disseminata et voce simul large lateque diffusa, qua cives omnes adlocutus est: quod tanto studio, tanta erga populum universum sollicitudine perfecit ut laudatione Enniana dignus sit:

Rex populo solus vigilando restituit rem:

NOS ERGO cum propter humanitatem eius studiorumque nostrorum cognitionem (nam inter silvas academicas ipse Matriti versatus est), tum propter diligentiam eius Europae totius conglutinandae causa strenue enitentis (quam ob rem praemio nomine Caroli Magni insigni honestatus est) in frequenti Congregationis Domo praedictum Regem DOCTOREM in Iure Civili renuntiamus eumque vi ac virtute huius Diplomatis omnibus iuribus et privilegiis adficimus quae ad hunc gradum spectant.

IN CVIVS REI TESTIMONIVM sigillum Vniversitatis quo hac in parte utimur adponendum curavimus.

Datum in Domo nostra Congregationis die XXIV° mensis Aprilis A.S. MCMLXXXVI.

HIS MAJESTY DON JUAN CARLOS I, KING OF SPAIN

THE CHANCELLOR, MASTERS, AND SCHOLARS
OF THE UNIVERSITY OF OXFORD
TO WHOMSOEVER THESE PRESENTS SHALL COME
MAY THE LORD EVER PRESERVE
AND KEEP YOU

WHEREAS it has long been our custom to show such particular honour as is in our power to distinguished Kings and Princes who have won fame by their fine character and their brave acts, especially those who are related to our own Royal House:

AND WHEREAS His Majesty Don Juan Carlos I, King of Spain, grandson of the illustrious Alfonso XIII who gave great encouragement and support to Spanish studies at Oxford (whereby our Professor of Spanish Studies enjoys the title *Alfonso XIII*), has from the time when he became King worked hard to create harmony among the diverse political parties and regions in Spain:

AND WHEREAS there is virtually no member of our Congregation who does not recall the 1981 conspiracy against the Spanish constitution, and in particular that memorable night of 23 February when, confronted with a military coup which had laid siege to the Parliament, while the force of law had been silenced by force of arms, King Juan Carlos alone preserved the constitution by sending immediate orders to his provincial commanders to keep their troops in barracks and by appearing on television with a message to his nation: which he has accomplished with such devotion to duty and such care for his whole people that he deserves praise in the language of Ennius:

Only the King's exertions preserved the state for all:

NOW THEREFORE WE, bearing in mind both his interest in the liberal arts and his familiarity with our studies (for he has himself experienced the atmosphere of a University in Madrid) and also his energetic devotion to the cause of European cooperation, recognised in 1982 by the award of the Charlemagne Prize, do here in this full House of Congregation proclaim the aforesaid King a DOCTOR in our Faculty of Civil Law, and by power and virtue of this Diploma do hereby invest him with all privileges and rights of this Degree.

IN WITNESS WHEREOF we have caused to be affixed to this instrument the Seal of the University thereunto pertaining.

Given in our House of Congregation on the twenty-fourth day of April in the Year of Salvation 1986.

EMINENTISSIMVS CARDINALIS AVGVSTINVS CASAROLI

PAPA *iste tuus, quot habet legiones?* hoc contumeliose interroganti Iosepho isti adamantino nunc demum decet respondere. legiones certe non habet Papa Sanctissimus, habet tamen legationes; quae momentum haud exiguum contulerunt ad Russos populosque Europae orientalis cum Americanis gentibusque Europae citerioris in concordiam nuper adducendos. cuius concordiae renascentis praenuntium nunc produco: adest Cardinalis Eminentissimus qui abhinc triginta annos legatus a Papa Vindobonam missus est, Aquincum deinde, Pragam Singidunum Varsaviam Moscoviam, ad Helsingenses Berolinenses Bonnenses Cubanos Americanos Mexicanos Helvetios Argentinos . . . *quo fessum rapitis?* licet ei certe versum illum ab Aenea in Africa pronuntiatum repetere:

> quae regio in terris nostri non plena laboris?

diu enim a comitatu exiguo adiutus concordiae fundamenta paulatim construit.

Romae autem Papae est consiliarius sagax et fortis, qui edicta Concili Vaticani Secundi libenter exsequitur, ecclesiae gentium singularum auctoritatem quam maximam dandam esse censet. in legationibus agendis verbis utitur apertis et sinceris, nam sinceritatem et simplicitatem prae se fert, haud tamen desunt artes oratori propriae. optime enim cognovit legati proprium officium esse indagare *quid possit oriri.* quae artes, quae conscientia multum ei profuerunt Ecclesiae Sanctae legato identidem misso ad populos principesque impios qui Ecclesiae eiusdem sacerdotes vexabant atque insectabantur. erant certe qui talia a Legato Papae Sanctissimi vituperanda tantum esse censebant. ecce tamen nunc videtis omnes quid consiliis lenioribus et humanioribus adsequi potuerit. multis quidem legatus talis videtur esse qui dominis conciliandis populis ad orientem sitis nec non Ecclesiae suae prodesse studuerit; malim egomet loqui de humanitate huius aperta.

Humanitatem eandem in studiis quae otiosus exercet invenietis: musicorum qui classici vocantur operibus maxime delectatur. rerum gestarum libros interdum legit; nec non iuvenes quosdam Romae educandos curat, quibus ipse minister atque adiutor adest.

Praesento vobis legatum Ecclesiae Catholicae et Romanae peritissimum, Cardinalem Eminentissimum, Augustinum Casaroli, ut admittatur honoris causa ad gradum Doctoris in Sacra Theologia.

14

CARDINAL AGOSTINO CASAROLI
Vatican ambassador

THE *Pope! How many divisions has* he *got?* Now is a suitable time to answer this contemptuous question once put by Stalin, the Man of Steel. The Pope has indeed got no legions, but he has legations; and these have made a big contribution to the recent establishment of friendly relations between Russia and the peoples of Eastern Europe and the United States and the countries of Western Europe. The honorand whom I now present was a harbinger of these friendly relations: here is His Eminence Cardinal Casaroli, who was sent thirty years ago by the Pope to Vienna, and thereafter to Budapest, Prague, Belgrade, Warsaw, Moscow, Helsinki, Berlin, Bonn, Cuba, America, Mexico, Switzerland, Argentina . . . *quo fessum rapitis?* – the long list is itself exhausting. He has a right to quote what Aeneas said in Africa:

> Where in the world do men not see our work?

For a long time with a tiny staff he has been laying the foundations for good relations.

In Rome he is a wise and fearless counsellor of the Pope, happy to carry out the decisions of the Second Vatican Council and in favour of delegating as much power as possible to the individual Catholic Churches of different nations. As a diplomat he speaks openly and sincerely, indeed his sincerity and simplicity shine forth, and yet he is skilled in diplomatic technique, for he is well aware that the task of an ambassador is to work out what is practicable – the Art of the Possible. This awareness and these diplomatic skills were of particular advantage on the various occasions when he was sent to represent the Holy See in countries with godless regimes which persecuted the ministers of the Church. Some critics believed that a Papal legate should confine himself to denouncing and censuring such persecution. Now, however, you can all see plainly what our honorand has achieved by gentler methods and the exercise of great humanity. There is much talk of his *Ostpolitik,* but I would rather speak of his manifest humanity.

This humanity is apparent also in Cardinal Casaroli's other enthusiasms, classical music and historical writers. In addition, he exercises a pastoral ministry among the young people at the State Centre for the Re-education of Minors in Rome.

I present a most experienced ambassador of the Church of Rome, His Eminence Cardinal Agostino Casaroli, for the Honorary Degree of Doctor of Divinity.

1991

15

NIRAD CHANDRA CHAUDHURI

MEMINISTIS fortasse carmen vetus Indicum a me nuper repetitum: Bengallenses laudavit poeta utpote qui in disciplinis dialecticis et in arte poetica ingenio praestarent. Bengallensem nunc illustrissimum produco, poetarum nostrorum nec non Europaeorum valde peritum, qui Indorum mores atque consuetudines nobis ingenio maximo interpretatus est, nonnulla etiam quae in civitate nostra fiunt illustravit.

Natus autem prope pagum avitum Banagram a patre sagacissimo educatus est. φίλαγγλος erat, ut qui exemplis Britannorum clarissimorum puer exercitatus esset, quos in ordinem heroicum extollebat, Reginae scilicet nostrae Victoriae, Iohannis Milton, Arturi ducis de Wellington, Edmundi Burke, Indorum iniuria laborantium propugnatoris, ceterorumque virorum praeclarorum quorum verba nonnunquam aptissime laudat. etenim in libris duobus quos de vita sua scripsit luculenter explicavit quo modo vel puer vel adolescens moribus adfinium paganorumque imbutus esset, adfectus idem esset admiratione magna litterarum Anglicarum atque auctoritatis imperii Britannici.

Alumnus est insignis Universitatis Calcuttensis, ubi studia historica fecit. sinceritate autem mira de rebus quas ibi prospere gessit, nec non de repulsis scripsit. apud Dellienses postea electus est qui voce per aethera longe lateque proicienda res memorabiles populo toti exponeret.

> Et quando uberior tantarum copia rerum?

per vitam hic longinquam bella duo vidit per orbem saevissime grassantia, potestatem imperi Britannici sensim deminutam, libertatem tandem Indis conlatam, Indiam simul in partes duas divisam, tumultu tormentis trucidatione permultorum maculatam.

Res Indicas quas exponit se tamquam longe remotum desuper prospicere scripsit, ita tamen ut proximus eisdem maneat, in modum currus aerii circumvolitantis vel Mercuri illius Vergiliani

> avi similis qui circum litora, circum
> piscosos scopulos humilis volat aequora iuxta.
> haud aliter terras inter caelumque volabat.

Quibus de rebus sententiam pronuntiabat, candore forsitan maiore usus quam ut civibus suis placeret, quippe qui quaedam sub imperio nostro facta nimis laudaret, Indiae novae nascenti non satis faveret. sed labentibus annis magni iam apud suos aestimatur. qui *Indum* se *ignotum* olim appellavit famam praeclarissimam merito adsecutus est.

Libros hic libellosque multos edidit. vitas in primis duas doctissime conscripsit, cum Roberti Clive, ab India nominati, tum Maximi Mueller, Professoris Oxoniensis, qui studia linguae antiquae Indorum magnopere provexit. ad Angliam tandem anno quinquagesimo octavo advectus, quidquid hic per mensem unum gesserat ingeniose explicavit in libro multo sale condito, cui titulum *Iter Anglicum* per iocum dedit. quid plura? iam annos viginti apud nos versatus Oxoniensis factus est.

Praesento vobis Niradum Chandram Chaudhuri, Societatis Regiae Litteratorum Socium, qui Indos plurimos, plurimos Anglos docuit delectavit stimulavit, ut admittatur honoris causa ad gradum Doctoris in Litteris.

NIRAD CHANDRA CHAUDHURI
Writer

YOU may perhaps recall a Sanskrit poem which I once quoted, praising Bengalis for their outstanding ability in logic and poetry. The eminent Bengali whom I now present is thoroughly versed in both English and European poetry, and has interpreted Indian society and customs to us with great intellectual ability, illuminating incidentally several aspects of our own society.

Nirad Chaudhuri was born near Banagram, his ancestral village, and was educated by a wise father. He was an Anglophile, brought up as a boy on the examples of famous Britons whom he regarded as his heroes: Queen Victoria, Milton, Wellington, Burke, the champion of the oppressed people of India, and other great men whose words he quotes on suitable occasions. In his two volumes of autobiography he has vividly described how as a boy and a young man he was both steeped in the customs of his relations and the neighbouring villagers and influenced by a great admiration for English literature and the authority of the British Raj.

He is a graduate of the famous University of Calcutta, where he studied History. He writes with remarkable frankness of his successes and reverses there. He then worked as a radio commentator in Delhi, giving regular broadcasts on events of significance.

And when was there a richer crop?

During his long life he has seen two world wars, a gradual reduction in the power of the British Empire, freedom for India eventually achieved, and his country partitioned and harassed by riots, torture, and massacres.

In the preface to his *Autobiography* he tells us that when explaining events in India he has the advantage of a distant perspective without losing his closeness to those events – like a hovering aeroplane or Virgil's Mercury, messenger of the Gods, who is

> Like a bird flying low around the shores,
> Around the fishy rock-pools just above the sea.
> Even so he flew balanced between the earth and heaven.

Mr. Chaudhuri expressed his views on contemporary events with a frankness which was too great to make him popular with his fellow-Indians, praising certain aspects of the former Raj, and lacking in the requisite enthusiasm for the birth of the New India. But with the passage of time his reputation at home is now restored. The 'Unknown Indian' of his book has deservedly won fame and recognition.

He has published many books and articles, in particular two scholarly biographies dealing with Clive of India and Max Müller, the Oxford Professor who gave great impetus to the study of Sanskrit. He visited England eventually in his fifty-eighth year, and brilliantly related his adventures during a month here in a book spiced with wit, which he mischievously entitled *Passage to England*. The outcome is that he is already now an Oxonian, having lived among us for twenty years.

I present Nirad Chandra Chaudhuri, FRSL, who has instructed, delighted, and stimulated great numbers of Indians and English people, for the Honorary Degree of Doctor of Letters.

1990

LEONARDVS CHESHIRE

OXONIENSEM primum produco insignem, patre Oxoniensi insigni natum, cuius nomen apud iuris consultos magnam etiam nunc habet auctoritatem. ipse tamen omnibus olim ideo notissimus erat quod alae isti aëriae sescentesimae decimae septimae praefectus erat, quae fulmina belli pondere inaudito congesta per ingentes caeli tractus portata in hostium armamentaria et officinas noctu accuratissime coniecit. cuius accurationis testes adfero matres familiarum quingentas Lemovicum, quae ad aetatem iam optatam idcirco pervenerunt quod cum officinam in qua laborabant delevit ipsas summa cura servavit. pari sollertia nostris subveniendi causa montem totum prope Ligerem fluvium Neptuni more evertit. quid plura? Cruce Victoriana honoratus est, quae insignia cetera splendore fortitudinis praestringit,

Post bellum caede nefanda vexatus aliquid auxili hominibus cupiebat adferre, itaque eos adiuvare constituit qui aegritudine tali laborarent ut valetudinariis publicis emittendi essent. villae ad hoc faciendum comparatae iam exstant fere ducentae viginti per orbem terrarum, *domus* appellatae et nomine huius insignes. o rem magnam et laboriosam! ecce γενναίων ἀρεταὶ πόνων quae ἄγαλμα quoddam felicitatis viro generoso praestant. immo vero verba licet repetere quae de fortissimis huius commilitonibus olim audivimus: rarissime viro uni tanta tot homines beneficia debuerunt.

Consilia haec ei incommodis permultis impedita perficienti adiutrix aderat coniunx promptissima, de rebus talibus maxime perita, quae eos qui belli vicibus adflicti erant adiuvandos curabat, domorum ipsa fundatrix. domos autem suas ea mente instituit ut eis subveniret qui in loco quoque valetudine inopiaque vexarentur, incolis eiusdem regionis adiuvantibus. nempe in animo habebat ut victus invalidis et cura suppeditarentur ei simillima quam pater familias liberis alumnisque adsidue praeberet. etenim domibus praefecti tam bene res quibus egeant invalidi cognoverunt ut hoc exemplo rationem totam tales curandi meliorem fecerint.

Ne tamen putetis ratione has et consilio νομοθετῶν severiorum institutas esse, libros quos conscripsit legite. invenietis domum eum primam instituisse amici aegerrimi inopia impulsum, quem sua ipse manu usque ad mortem curavisset, alios deinde inopia urgente recepisse. humanitate igitur et voluntate singulos adiuvandi res tota nititur. adest enim qui virtutibus a Domino nostro laudatis adfectus est, atque adeo Caritate ipsa quae earum est maxima.

Praesento vobis Leonardum Cheshire, e Collegio Mertonensi, Cruce Victoriana honoratum, Ordini insigniter Meritorum adscriptum, ut admittatur honoris causa ad gradum Doctoris in Iure Civili.

LEONARD CHESHIRE
Founder of Cheshire Homes

THE first honorand is an Oxford man, son of a distinguished Oxford lawyer; Cheshire on *Real Property* is still quoted with great respect. Forty years ago, however, virtually everybody in Britain knew the name Cheshire, for our honorand Leonard Cheshire had been given command of 617 Squadron, Bomber Command, which transported enormous bombs packed with explosive long distances into enemy territory; these they delivered by night with great precision on enemy installations and arms factories. I can call five hundred witnesses to testify to the precision of their attacks. They are women living in Limoges who have survived to become mothers and grandmothers because of the accuracy with which Group Captain Cheshire destroyed the aero-engine factory where they were working during the war. He displayed equal ability in 1944 when he played the part of Neptune and annihilated an entire hill by the Loire to give protection to our invading forces. His work with 617 Squadron is summed up by the award of a Victoria Cross, the decoration which puts all other medals in the shade.

After the war Leonard Cheshire, distressed by the appalling loss of life, wanted to do something positive to help people. He decided to aid disabled patients who were suffering from illnesses which could not be treated in hospital. There are now some two hundred and twenty Cheshire Homes throughout the world. This great achievement needed much hard work:

> O bienheureux travail d'un esprit glorieux.

Indeed we may describe it in words which we once heard applied to his colleagues in Fighter Command: seldom has so much been owed by so many to one man.

His plans were hindered by considerable obstacles. As he put them into execution he had the active support and advice of his wife, Sue Ryder, who was experienced in this field, as an organizer of help for the victims of the war, a Founder of Homes herself. The Cheshire Homes were started to meet the needs of their various localities, and they depend on local support. They aim 'to provide care and shelter in an atmosphere as close as possible to that of a family'. They have treated the disabled with such sensitivity to their needs that they have set an example which has improved the treatment of disabled people everywhere.

Do not imagine that Leonard Cheshire's Homes are the result of the exact planning of a social scientist. Just read his books and you will discover that he started the first Home because of the pressing need of a sick friend, whom he himself tended right up to his death. He took in other patients because of the urgency of their need. The whole structure of the Homes is founded on humanity, the desire to help individual men and women. Here is a man motivated by the Christian virtues, and by the greatest of these, which is Love.

I present Leonard Cheshire, VC, OM, of Merton College, for admission to the Honorary Degree of Doctor of Civil Law.

1984

IACQUELINA DU PRÉ

σκιᾶς ὄναρ
ἄνθρωπος· ἀλλ᾽ ὅταν αἴγλα διόσδοτος ἔλθῃ,
λαμπρὸν φέγγος ἔπεστιν ἀνδρῶν καὶ μείλιχος αἰών.

CLARIS huic ingeni luminibus praeditae splendor quidam a dis immortalibus donatus accessit, qui in prima iuventute exarsit. conventibus enim frequentissimis qui tetrachordon eam modulantem audiebant varietas sonorum mirabilis suppeditabatur:

tot fuerant illic quot habet Natura colores.

Omnes autem qui tali praestantia eminent ad orbem terrarum universum pertinent. recte tamen hanc sibi homines Angli vindicant. Oxoniae enim nata, a Gulielmo Pleeth docta, Londini educata est, Londiniensibus primo artem suam exposuit, studia deinde foris apud viros insignissimos, Casals Tortelier Rostropovich, exercuit.

Tetrachordo suo per lustra fere tria plurimos delectabat; neque musicae artis iudicibus solum, durissimo generi, placebat, sed turbae etiam nostrum minus doctorum qui optima gaudemus audientes cordi maxime erat. quanti quondam animi motus et audientibus et intuentibus obferebantur qui hanc lyramque eius coniunctione cum laetissima tum etiam validissima conflatas sentiebant. etenim si quis carmen illud ab Eduardo nostro, auctore maxime Anglico, compositum, de morte iuvenum nostrorum pro patria recens occisorum dolente, fidibus huius Anglicae apud Anglos eruditae cum concentu maximo cithararum tibiarumque cantatam audivit, quid sit amor patriae ingens et iustissimus optime cognovit.

At nunc dormitat decus illud. gloriae tamen vivida est vis,

αἱ δὲ τεαὶ ζώουσιν ἀηδόνες

discis filisque summa cura conservatae. fama etiam apud medicos permanet qui nomine huius adiuti causas et remedia morborum indagant. permanet quoque exemplum fortitudinis et tranquillitatis quod ceteris nempe succurrit qui valetudine eadem opprimuntur.

Praesento vobis Musis amicam, Iacquelinam du Pré, Excellentissimo Ordini Imperii Britannici adscriptam, ut admittatur honoris causa ad gradum Doctoris in Musica.

JACQUELINE DU PRÉ
Musician

Man's but a shadow in a dream;
But when God sends a bright heroic gleam
We hail the holy light, and life is sweet as honey.

OUR honorand was born with great natural talent. This was enhanced by a splendour which blazed forth in her early youth. The great audiences which heard her playing the 'cello encountered a wonderful variety of sounds:

All colours that the earth creates were there.

Artists who display such excellence belong to the whole world; but the people of England rightly claim Jacqueline du Pré as English. She was born in Oxford, taught by William Pleeth, and educated at the Guildhall School of Music; and she gave her first concert performances in London before going abroad to study with the great masters, Casals, Tortelier, Rostropovich.

For more than a decade she gave joy to large assemblies. Appreciation of her work was not confined to the severe world of the serious musical critics: the ordinary public of non-professionals, who enjoy listening to the best, took her to their hearts. To hear and to watch Jacqueline du Pré fused with her 'cello in a joyful, vigorous union was a very moving experience. The audiences who listened to this musician, born and trained in England, playing the 'cello concerto of Elgar, that most English of composers, written to express his grief for our young men who died for their country, knew what it was to feel a deep and true patriotism.

But some man will say, 'Thy former splendour now slumbereth'. But not the praise, for that endures:

Still are thy nightingales awake,

preserved and on record. The fame of our honorand is also still active in the Jacqueline du Pré Research Fund for Multiple Sclerosis and in the example she gives of bravery and serenity, which is an encouragement and aid for all those who suffer from this complaint.

I present Jacqueline du Pré, OBE, musician, for admission to the Honorary Degree of Doctor of Music.

1984

EDVARDVS EAST

ΓΛΑΥΚ' Ἀθήναζε dicebant antiqui si quis *Cereri sua dona merumque Lyaeo* reddiderat. adest honoris causa vir honorum peritissimus, qui diu graduum academicorum conferendorum pars magna fuit, ut ipse ad gradum admittatur.

Mariscalcus hic academicus per annos XIV fuit, quem vidimus omnes saepe illustrissimos viros feminasque, Reges aliquando Praesidesque, summa dexteritate in hoc theatro disponentem, in ordine quemque suo instructos. nec minore sollertia viatores lictoresque disponebat. praecipuum autem hoc ei officium fuit ut Procuratoribus ab epistulis esset, quibus exempla vel decreta Procuratorum priorum tam apte proferebat ut machinis computatricibus vix opus esset: tali memoria, tanta peritia praeditus erat. etenim virum prudentissimum produco, secretorum plurimorum conscium, de quibus mihi non licet more solito oratorum disserere – βοῦς ἐπὶ γλώσσῃ μέγας / βέβηκε.

Non mirum est eum nuper a Procuratoribus Assessoribusque permultis quos adiuvaverat epulis amplissimis honestatum esse. nam viri complures in Universitate nostra praestantissimi tirocinium in rebus academicis agendis egerunt Mariscalco hoc docente, ut qui propositi istius summi Universitatis semper tenax fuerit, ut disciplinae academicae semper excolantur. audite quaeso laudationem eximiam a Procuratoribus recentioribus scriptam: 'cui consilium identidem dedit Eduardus noster, studiis hic liberalibus instructus est.'

Omnibus quos adloquebatur, sive Procuratoribus sive lictoribus, sermone comitatis atque adeo adfabilitatis pleno utebatur – salva tamen dignitate officii sui, quam in caeremoniis manifeste praestabat. Procuratorum autem lictoribus et ministris epulas quotannis curavit instituendas, Encaeniis rite peractis dum Cancellarius virique nuper honorati hospitio gratissimo Collegii Omnium Animarum fruebantur. ecce ingenium maxime versatile: Procuratorum infantes libenter custodivit; prandium ipse comparavit (nam artis coquendi est peritus) quod cum Procuratoribus in loco amoeno sub divo comesset; Cancellarium illum τὸν μακαρίτην iam seniorem benignissime adiuvit; piscem quondam istum fabulosum, cyprinum Nipponensem curavit.

Tirocinium ipse Mariscalco aptum egerat, vigiliis adscriptus quae urbem nostram custodiunt, εὐδόντων ὕπερ / ἐγρηγορὸς φρούρημα. Mariscalcus igitur creatus saluti academicorum praecipue consuluit, vigilias nocturnas ipse curavit agendas, custodes perpetuos in officina sua instituit.

Quid plura? Eduardum East praesento, qui beneficia sescenta non modo Procuratoribus multis sed etiam Universitati toti largitus est, ut admittatur honoris causa ad gradum Magistri in Artibus.

EDWARD EAST
University Marshal

'OWLS to Athens' was the proverb used by the ancients whenever somebody gave back

> To Ceres her own gifts and wine to Bacchus.

Here to be honoured is an expert in honours, who played a large part in the conferring of degrees and is now himself to receive a degree.

Mr East was University Marshal for fourteen years. We have all seen him tactfully marshalling distinguished men and women, sometimes Kings and Presidents, making sure that each was in his proper station. As Marshal he deployed his Bedels and Bulldogs with equal skill. But his principal task was to act as Secretary to the Proctors and provide them with apt precedents or rulings by their predecessors. For this he needed no computer; such were his own experience and his memory. Our honorand is the soul of discretion, for he is privy to a great many secrets about which I am not permitted to discourse as orators are wont to do: I have a 'great ox on my tongue' just like the Watchman in *Agamemnon*.

It is no wonder that on his recent retirement the many Proctors and Assessors he had helped honoured him with a banquet. For a fair number of prominent people in our University served their apprenticeship in university administration under the tutelage of Mr East, a Marshal who always kept in sight the main academic function of a University. I quote a remarkable tribute to him written by some recent Proctors: 'To be advised by Ted East is to receive an education'.

In his dealings with everybody, from Proctors to Bulldogs, his style of speech was informal and kindly, but never so as to compromise the dignity of his office, which came out most evidently in University ceremonies. He instituted an annual feast for the Proctors' staff just after Encaenia, while the Chancellor and honorands were enjoying the welcome hospitality of an All Souls luncheon. His nature was indeed versatile: he has cheerfully acted as a baby-sitter for the Proctors; he has prepared picnics – for he is an expert cook – for consumption on his expeditions with the Proctors; he has given kindly help to our former Chancellor in his old age; he has looked after the strange fish we received from Japan, the koy carp.

He served his own apprenticeship – one appropriate for a Marshal – with the local Police, the custodians of this City, who 'guard our sleeping watchfully'. When he became Marshal he paid special attention to the security of the University, taking on the direction of the night patrol and setting up a 24-hour security section in the Proctors' office.

I need not elaborate further: I present Mr Edward East, who has conferred a great number of benefits on the Proctors and moreover on our whole University, for the Honorary Degree of Master of Arts.

1991

GERAINT EVANS

'POTIONES ecce cunctis, en salutem vendito!' Adest re vera Dulcamara iste medicus, qui se iam mercis suae institorem praestitit in hoc theatro academico. quot et qualia sub toga huius lateant medicamina quae mox proferat, vix enumerare ausim. scitote eum remedium amoris Principi suo Carolo impertivisse; cur dubitabit eadem Procuratoribus egregiis largiri? partes illas Dulcamarae ultimas egit cum in Odeo nostro hortensio nuper rude donatus est. tum mortuo plausu id maxime decuit animosque omnium maxime movit quod illi qui audiverant statim ei responderunt laudibus patriae eius lingua Cambrensi cantandis.

Magnopere doleo egomet nefas esse mihi carmen hic Cambrense cantare. laudes tamen quas impertio latine loqui more maiorum decet, repentes quidem per humum et cum praeconio isto vix comparandas. quo modo enim sermone meo pedestri vim et vigoris talis histrionis valebo depingere si partes tantum enumerabo quas cecinit? personarum praesertim comicarum memor sum, sive Domini Pasquale sive Papageni, qui labris sera conclusis aliquid tamen vociferabatur; sive Iohannis Falstaff, equitis scilicet comici in quo vis quaedam tragica inerat – vestimentum piri modo formatum habentis et misericordiam nobis praebentis cum ludibria ceterorum defendit laetitiam commemorando quam ipse ceteris praebuerat:

> vobis ego ipse plurimos feci iocos.

talia non possunt bene exprimi nisi ab histrione strenuo et mentis alacritate maxima praedito.

Etenim partibus quas clarissime in fabellis musicis egit quanta suberat cura, quanta de rebus minutissimis diligentia, laboris quantum improbi! nonne calceos constrictos ultro sumebat partes Beckmesseri acturus, ut subiratus in scaenam procederet? calceos idem laxos partes Wozzeki acturus, ut rustici incessum imitaretur. 'abeunt pedes in mores', dixit ipse. quam ad fabellam agendam morem cantandi solitum dediscere debebat ut artem novam παρακαταλογῇ similem disceret; id quod invitus fecit, animos tamen audientium graviter commovit.

Patria huius est terra illa prope Cardiffam sita quae a metallariis habitata est. studia autem grammaticorum anno quinto decimo invitus omisit ut Mercuriolus fieret, vocis deinde virtutibus colendis famam paulatim adeptus est. Londini apud Hortos frequentissime per triginta annos cantavit, et foris saepe partes egit, Mediolani, Salisburgi, Vindobonae, in America utraque. domi quoque nonnumquam apud penates nostros honoratissimos effigiem eius vivam vidimus. patriae tamen suae eorumque ex quibus ortus est minime est oblitus, qui uxorem habet egregiam in eadem regione natam, laetitiarum quondam iuvenilium participem.

Praesento vobis Geraint Evans, Equitem Auratum, Musis amicum, Collegii Iesu honoris causa Socium, ut admittatur honoris causa ad gradum Doctoris in Musica.

SIR GERAINT EVANS
Singer

> La salute a vendere
> Per tutto il mondo io vo.

HERE is the true, the genuine Doctor Dulcamara, ready to hawk his wares in the Sheldonian Theatre. Heaven knows what medicines he has concealed beneath his gown, ready to pull out and sell. You may know that he has already dispensed a love potion to the Prince of Wales; why should he hesitate to give a similar favour to the Proctors? Dulcamara was the final part which Sir Geraint Evans sang at his farewell performance last year at Covent Garden. After the applause had subsided the audience responded in a fitting and moving way: they sang to him the praise of his native land in Welsh.

I much regret that the rules of this ceremony do not permit me to sing in Welsh. The praise I give him must be in spoken Latin, earthbound indeed by comparison with that fine tribute. How can I in ordinary prose convey the spirit of such an actor by listing the parts he has sung? One thinks of him most naturally in his comic roles, as Don Pasquale or Papageno, trying to sing through a padlock; or as Falstaff, that comic knight in whom there is more than a hint of tragedy, in his ridiculous pear-shaped costume pathetically defending himself from ridicule by the pleasure he has given:

> Son' io che vi fa scaltri.

This was a part both physically and intellectually demanding.

Behind all his grand effects was minute attention to detail and hard – indeed excessive – work. Here is a man who deliberately wore tight shoes when singing Beckmesser because they made him irritable on stage, and large boots for Wozzeck to give the effect of a peasant's clumping walk. 'Character begins from the feet up', as he puts it. His performance of Wozzeck showed great versatility: he was prepared to unlearn the traditions of Grand Opera and learn the strange technique of *Sprechgesang*. This he did reluctantly, but his performance was most moving and effective.

He comes from the mining country near Cardiff. He had to leave school at the age of fourteen to take on the job of errand-boy. It was by diligent training of his voice that he gradually acquired a reputation. He has appeared most frequently at Covent Garden during the last thirty years and has often sung abroad, at Milan, Salzburg, Vienna, and in America, North and South. He has also appeared occasionally in our own household shrines on the television programmes, and yet he is not in the least inclined to forget his country and his origins; indeed his wife comes from the same parts and they grew up together there.

I present Sir Geraint Evans, musician, Honorary Fellow of Jesus College, for admission to the Honorary Degree of Doctor of Music.

1985

GARRET FITZGERALD

DUBLINENSEM Dublinensis produco, quem ego ceterique Hibernenses *Taoiseach* quondam vocavimus, omnium *Taoisigh* certe benignissimum. academicus est qui rei publicae praefectus de sermone patrio libellum docte nuper conscripsit. οἰκονομικῆς quoque est peritus, et arte et usu exercitatus. cum vero aliis per rationem adhibitam persuadere cupiat, disputandi est amantissimus, qui cum de rebus gravissimis agitur ad sermonem producendum paratus sit *dum defluat amnis;* quod huic fortasse ex usu fuit cum Ministris Britannicis rem agenti.

Benevolentia autem eum plurimi complectuntur, sive fautores sunt sive adversarii. nonne cognomine *Probi* a populo suo honoratus est? o virum felicem, cui Dublinenses, homines acutissimi et malevolentiae haud ignari, nihil contumeliosius per ludibrium obiecerunt! nempe cavendum est mihi ne nimium eum laudem, cui iam haud profuerit apud cives τοὺς ἐπιτυχόντας Hibernenses a scriptoribus Britannicis praeconiis plurimis ornari.

Et pater huius et mater, adiutrix haec Georgii Bernhardi Shaw, amicus ille Gulielmi Yeats, in numero coniuratorum fuerunt qui patriam olim in libertatem vindicaverunt. pater tandem civitatem novam dirigendam curavit, rebus exteris praefectus, quibus filius etiam hic annos abhinc quattuordecim praefectus est.

Praefecto mox contigit, Communitatis Europaeae olim fautori, Praesidi primo Hibernensi esse Concilii Ministrorum Europaeorum. Praeses vero multa insignite fecit edixitque quae patriae cum gentibus istis nuperrime consociatae laudi et gloriae fuerunt. illud ei praecipue expedivit quod linguam Francogallicam optime callet. haud scio an res hunc maximae maneant foris prospere gerendae.

Princeps tandem civitatis electus ad nodum paene inexplicabilem explicandum operam dedit. bene enim mentem ingeniumque cognoverat plurimorum partem borealem Hiberniae incolentium qui cives se Britannicos esse laetantur, regno huic quam maxime coniunctos. hos quamvis moribus valde diversos in concordiam ducere voluit, itaque post disputationes multas cum Reginae nostrae Ministris foedus iecit, ex quo colloquia statis temporibus nunc habent legati Dublinenses cum legatis Britannicis. nova haec coepta et prius inaudita, quibus in regione boreali multi adhuc adversantur. concordiae tamen causa laborantibus omnia bona fausta felicia fortunataque precamur.

Praesento vobis Garret FitzGerald, Hiberniae quondam *Taoiseach* creatum, Doctorem iam in Philosophia, Academiae Hibernensi Regali adscriptum, ut admittatur honoris causa ad gradum Doctoris in Iure Civili.

GARRET FITZGERALD
Taoiseach of Ireland

HERE you have a Dublin honorand, presented by a Dublin man. Dr Garret FitzGerald used to be known to us in Ireland as *Taoiseach,* surely the most good-humoured of all *Taoisigh.* He is an academic who recently while in office published a scholarly paper on the decline of the Irish language. He has been a professional economist, with practical knowledge of the subject. Since he wants to persuade people by rational means, he has a taste for discussion. About things that really matter he is prepared to talk till the Liffey runs dry, a facility which has perhaps helped him in his negotiations with British Ministers.

He enjoys a great fund of goodwill from political opponents as well as from his supporters. At home he has been called 'Garret the Good'. It is an achievement worthy of congratulation to have been slandered in this comparatively mild way by the citizens of Dublin, who are a sharp-witted and sharp-tongued populace. Indeed I must be careful to be moderate in my praise of Dr FitzGerald; for in the past the great praise he has had from the British press has done him no good with the Plain People of Ireland.

His father, Desmond FitzGerald, was a friend of W. B. Yeats; his mother worked for a time with George Bernard Shaw. Both of them took part in the Easter Rising. Thereafter Desmond FitzGerald worked to govern the new Irish state. He became Minister for External Affairs, an office to which his son Garret was appointed in 1973.

As a long-standing supporter of the European Community, it was particularly appropriate that our honorand was elected the first Irish President of the Council of Ministers of the Community. During his Presidency his acts and speeches, and not least his fluency in French, enhanced the reputation of Ireland, which had but recently joined the Community. Who knows what triumphs of international statesmanship may still await him?

When he became head of the Government he devoted himself to the solution of a problem which is almost insoluble. He had previously acquired an unusual understanding of the position and feelings of the Unionist majority in Northern Ireland, who are proud to be British citizens and value their close connection with this country. Despite the fact that they belong to a different tradition, he was anxious to achieve a reconciliation with them. After long discussions with the British Government he signed an 'Anglo-Irish Agreement', as a result of which there are now regular meetings between British Ministers and officials and their Dublin counterparts. This is a novel initiative; there are still many Northerners hostile to it. But we earnestly wish that success may crown the efforts of those who work for the cause of peace.

I present Dr Garret FitzGerald, MRIA, formerly *Taoiseach* of Ireland, for the Honorary Degree of Doctor of Civil Law.

1987

ELISABETHA FRINK

FACILLIME eadem consentimus nosmet aequalesque nostri cum Atheniensibus illis orbatis de quibus a Pericle quondam dictum est:

ἐν πολυτρόποις ξυμφοραῖς ἐπίστανται τραφέντες.

etenim memoria temporis nostri inquieti gravissime adficimur si quando signa ab hac quam praesento fabricata attentius intuemur. adsidue enim in mentem venit versus notissimus Vergilianus:

sunt lacrimae rerum et mentem mortalia tangunt.

Ecce homines pennati qui semper altius ad solem enituntur in modum Icari. corpus istud spectate per aëra cadentis. aspicite viris his currentibus vis quanta insit, capitibus illis ingentibus quantum robur, cum vi ista consili experti fortasse coniunctum. operibus nempe huius permultis subest nescio quid asperitatis. itaque haud inepte verba quaedam laudabo de Iacobo Epstein ab Oratore nostro quondam pronuntiata: 'mollia non curat excudere, sed fortia potius.' quod si quis indoctus tamquam errorem huic obiciat, aptissime possit iocum hunc Ciceronianum repetere: 'errare, mehercule, malo cum Platone.'

Gaudium vero maximum ceperunt iam plurimi, sive docti sive indocti, qui per viam quae ab Amore isto Londiniensi ducit spatiati signum ab hac factum subito aspexerunt equitis nobilis *fumum et opes strepitumque* viae illius celeberrimae contemplantis. neque tu, aper ferox inhabilisque ex aere ducte, indictus abibis, neque vos, equi formosi, hominibus huius anxiis placidiores. sed quia plura? quae nonnullis lacrimas expressit, laetitiam multis praestitit, nonne digna est quam in Theatro Sheldoniano honestemus?

Schelsegae artem didicit, Oxoniensis tamen iam est quae Collegii Sanctae Hildae Socia honoris causa creata sit. artifices haec alios auxilium petentes benigne atque comiter solet adiuvare, nec non discipulos nostros Oxonienses. officiis autem nonnullis functa est, annos abhinc quattuordecim Musei Britannici fiduciaria electa.

Unam denique precationem bona vestra cum venia addam, si forsitan adnuat sive deus sive auditor Oxoniensis pietate insignis et benevolentia. Iacobi illius illustrissimi quem olim honoravimus monumentum maximum in Collegio Novo, Lazarum scilicet nobilissimum, possumus frequentare. utinam opus aliquod ab hac Oxoniensi fictum Oxoniae situm Oxonienses aliquando delectet!

Praesento vobis Elisabetham Frink, Excellentissimi Ordinis Imperii Britannici Dominam Commendatricem, Academiae Regiae adscriptam, Collegii Sanctae Hildae Sociam honoris causa, ut admittatur honoris causa ad gradum Doctoris in Litteris.

DAME ELISABETH FRINK

Sculptor

MY contemporaries find it particularly easy to sympathize with the bereaved Athenians of whom Pericles said: 'They know that they have been reared in an age of startling vicissitudes.' We are most strongly affected by the recollection of our own troubled times when we look attentively at the sculpture of Dame Elisabeth Frink. A well-known line of Virgil keeps on coming to mind:

Matter is here for tears: things mortal touch the heart.

Here are winged men who are ever straining towards the sun like Icarus. Look at that body falling through the air. See the power inherent in these running men, the strength of those huge heads, which is perhaps combined with 'mindless force', as Horace put it. There is indeed a fundamental ruggedness in many of her works, which justifies me in quoting these words once used by our Orator in presenting Epstein for an honorary degree: 'His aim in sculpture is to create not smoothness but strength.' Should some inexperienced critic complain of this as a fault in our honorand, she could appropriately reply with Cicero's joke: 'I'd rather be at fault in company with Plato.'

Very many people, whether experienced or inexperienced in criticism, have felt great joy when, as they walk down Piccadilly from the Eros statue, they suddenly espy Elisabeth Frink's noble horseman contemplating that crowded street with all 'the din and fumes of town, the lushness of the Ritz'. And I cannot leave her bronze boar, so proud and clumsy, without a mention, nor her lovely horses, so tranquil by comparison with her troubled men. Need I say more? This artist, whose work has brought tears to some and pleasure to many, is indeed a fit person to be honoured in the Sheldonian Theatre.

She was trained at the Chelsea School of Art. Now as an Honorary Fellow of St Hilda's College she is already an Oxford woman. She is kindly and generous with her help when consulted by other artists, or indeed by our students. She has undertaken a number of public duties, and has been a Trustee of the British Museum for fourteen years.

Finally, if you will permit me, I would like to express one wish, in the hope that some god or some Oxonian in the audience with feelings of generosity and devotion to the University may assent to it. We have in New College a memorial to our honoured Epstein, his noble Lazarus, which we can visit. Would that Oxford had a work by this Oxford honorand to delight the Oxonians!

I present Dame Elisabeth Frink, DBE, RA, Honorary Fellow of St Hilda's College, for the Honorary Degree of Doctor of Letters.

1989

IOHANNES KENNETH GALBRAITH

ADEST oeconomicus saeculi nostri fere notissimus, cuius libros aliquot (late enim vulgati sunt) plurimi nostrum in armariis perlectos habemus. nam disciplinae suae quamvis peritissimus sit, de hominibus quibusdam vel singulis vel consociatis solet scribere. etenim *quidquid agunt homines,* materies illa poetae veteris, fundamentum certe subest scientiae toti oeconomicae. permulti tamen oeconomicorum, οἷοι νῦν εἰσι, rerum naturae scientiam se colere rati, mathematicis se simillimos esse censent, formulisque igitur arcanis verbisque quae profanis obscura sunt lectorum oculos praestringunt.

Legenti mihi iterum opera quaedam huius versus ille Terentianus in mentem venit:

homo sum: humani nil a me alienum puto.

itaque non mirum est haec ab academicis litterarum studiosis saepe perlegi. philologis in primis grata sunt; verba enim elegantissime componit lectorisque arbitrio consulit. audite quod scripsit ipse in epistula quam legatus ad Iohannem Kennedy misit:

taedium quoad potuimus vitandum curavimus.

verbis etiam nonnullis sermonem Anglicum ditavit, quorum exempla mox agnoscetis. vestimenta vero habet Doctoris in Iure Civili; aptissime tamen ad gradum Doctoris in Litteris admittamus.

Rationes autem multas ab oeconomicis prioribus excogitatas ab egestate dura natas esse docuit: civitates nunc plerasque quae rerum copia abundent rationibus valde diversis gubernari. etenim medicorum in modum indagavit quae mala insint civitate ubi cuique *quaerenda pecunia primum est.* remedia quaedam protulit: inopiam per medicinas certas esse avertendam, monopoliis etiam *vim,* ut dicit, *contrariam* in modum compensationis adponendam esse.

Libros plurimos edidit quorum titulis ipsis vis vivida inest: *De inopiae late patentis natura, De potentiae conformatione, De aetate hac* ἀβεβαίῳ *omnia dubitantium.* librum autem subtilem scripsit de tempore illo turbulento cum apud transatlanticos pretia omnium casu tanto ceciderunt ut prorsus iacerent. experientia vero res oeconomicas doctus est, utpote qui rei publicae bellum gerenti operam multam contulisset, Praesidum deinde consiliarius electus esset, legatus etiam a Iohanne Kennedy apud Indos triennium habitavisset.

Praesento vobis oeconomicum consummatum, Iohannem Galbraith, Professorem in Universitate Harvardiana emeritum, ut admittatur honoris causa ad gradum Doctoris in Iure Civili.

JOHN KENNETH GALBRAITH
Economist

PROFESSOR Galbraith is virtually the best-known economist in modern times. His books have been widely published; most of us have some thumbed copies on our shelves. For despite his expertise in economic theory his practice is to write about specific people, whether as individuals or as members of a group. 'Whatever people do', the subject-matter of Juvenal, is surely the foundation which underlies the whole science of Economics. Yet many economists of the modern variety assume that they are practising not an art but a science; assimilating themselves to mathematicians, they dazzle their readers with mysterious formulae and jargon which is obscure to the uninitiated.

When I re-read my Galbraith books I was reminded of that famous line of Terence:

I am a man: I regard nothing that is human as alien to myself.

It is no wonder that these books of his are frequently read by scholars who are devoted to literature. They are especially pleasing to lovers of language, for he writes elegantly, paying regard to his reader's taste and judgment. I quote what he wrote as Ambassador in one of his letters to John Kennedy: 'I tried to avoid tedium.' He has, moreover, enriched the English language with a number of new phrases; you will recognize some instances in what follows. He is dressed in the robes of a Doctor of Civil Law, but we would be well justified in honouring him as a Doctor of Letters.

Professor Galbraith has maintained that many of the doctrines of previous economists arose in conditions of harsh poverty, whereas our modern affluent society is subject to very different forces and principles. He has diagnosed the diseases of an acquisitive economy and has prescribed certain remedies: various specific provisions to counter poverty and the applications of 'countervailing power' to regulate monopolies.

The very titles of his long list of books are stimulating: *The Nature of Mass Poverty*, *The Anatomy of Power, The Age of Uncertainty, The Great Crash*, a most subtle work. He learned his economics from hard experience: in 1941–5 he made a large contribution to the war effort; after the war he was appointed adviser to several Presidents, and he lived for three years in India as Kennedy's Ambassador.

I present an economist of the highest order, John Kenneth Galbraith, Professor Emeritus at Harvard University, for the Honorary Degree of Doctor of Civil Law.

1990

MURRAY GELL-MANN

ADEST vir qui non solum *inventor rerum* verissime salutari debet, sed etiam *inventor nominum*. raro enim academicorum rerum naturalium peritorum scripta laudantur in *Indice* nostro *Oxoniensi* verborum Anglicorum. hic est qui *quarces* adiuvantibus aliis invenit, inventasque nomine Dublinensi e libro illo obscurissimo Iacobi Joyce adhibito iocose appellavit. quod nomen si forte ignotum tibi est, *paucis (adverte) docebo*.

Apud Democritum Epicurumque primordia vel elementa rerum *atomi* erant; quas me puero diffindere valuerunt physici; itaque de *protis* atque *neutris* tum loquebamur. ecce tamen nunc particulae vel minores inventae sunt, quarces scilicet; quarum quaedam natura singulari praeditae *singulares* vel *alienae* vocantur. de mysteriorum arcanis nunc dissero, de quibus plura dicere mihi quidem non licet, secreto potius venerari. pro certo tamen scio verbum *singularitatem* hoc sensu adhibitum linguae nostrae ab hoc additum esse.

Itaque non mirum est hunc pronuntiasse se linguarum structurae oblectamenti causa studere. etenim studiis diversissimis operam dat, et historicis et biologicis. nonne artis etiam archaeometricae studiosus est? studium autem suum validissimum discendi aliis solet impertiri, ut qui disciplinas omnes artificum veneretur. quid multa? hunc in picturis licet intueri musicorum concentum dirigentem vel epulas lautissimas scienter et eleganter comparantem. librum etiam videtur composuisse ut quarces suas simplices cum bestiis saevissimis et multiplicibus comparet.

Professor est annos iam quinque et viginti in Instituto Technologico Californiae praestantissimo, Praemio Nobeliano honoratus, nec non nomismatibus praemiisque aliis ornatus. quod Institutum adeo ei placet ut diutissime in eo studia exerceat, blanditiis Harvardensium repulsis. nonne maxime *quarcis* hunc inventorem decet honorari ab hac Universitate unde carmen illud de *snarce* captanda quondam prolatum est?

Praesento vobis Murray Gell-Mann, ut admittatur honoris causa ad gradum Doctoris in Scientia.

MURRAY GELL-MANN
Physicist

HERE is an honorand who deserves a double salute, both as *scientific innovator* and as *verbal innovator*. Seldom are the writings of scientists cited in the *Oxford English Dictionary*. It was Professor Gell-Mann who in collaboration with other scientists discovered *quarks*, and went on to christen them in light-hearted fashion with a Dublin word taken from Joyce's most obscure work, *Finnegan's Wake*. If by chance you do not know the word, attend, and I will briefly instruct you.

In Democritus and Epicurus the first elements of material things were *atoms*. When I was a boy the physicists acquired the power to split these; and so we then used to talk about *protons* and *neutrons*. But now, lo and behold, even smaller sub-atomic particles have been discovered, *quarks* forsooth; and some of these, endowed with strange and unusual properties, are called *strange*. This lecture is now dealing with mystic secrets, of which I may not say more, but rather venerate them in silence. However, I know for sure that the word *strangeness* used in the sense indicated has been added to our language by Professor Gell-Mann.

No wonder, then, that he has listed 'linguistics' among his subsidiary interests. The subjects which claim his attention are indeed diverse, including both biological and historical topics. He even has an interest in archaeometrics. His strong enthusiasm for learning, covering all creative endeavour, is infectious. In short, you may inspect slides showing Murray Gell-Mann conducting a symphony or preparing an elaborate meal. It seems that he has even devised a book called *The Quark and the Jaguar,* comparing his simple quark with a highly-organized beast.

He has now been R. A. Millikan Professor of Theoretical Physics at the California Institute of Technology for twenty-five years. He is a Nobel Prizewinner, and has been awarded other Prizes and Medals. He is deeply attached to *Caltech,* where he has so long pursued his research, brushing aside the blandishments of Harvard. It is surely most appropriate that the inventor of the *quark* should be honoured by this University, which was the home of that epic *The Hunting of the Snark*.

I present Murray Gell-Mann for the Honorary Degree of Doctor of Science.

1992

GVLIELMVS GOLDING

QUORUM *pars magna fui,* dixit Aeneas. potuit dicere *quae sunt pars magna mei.* valent enim scripta huius motus animi impertire maximos, ut res ab alio gesta pars fiat lectoris, quam ossibus et venis potius quam mente sentiat, qui temporum illorum particeps ipse fiat 'quae tamquam fastigium vitae totius exstiterint'. inhaerescit enim in mente 'aliquid Leonidae' ab hoc traditum.

Librum autem notissimum ideo conscripsit quod malevolentia commotus erat quam hominibus ad humanitatem excultis subesse cognovit, per bellum nefandum clarissime manifestam:

> ecce apes mellis feraces, en ferax homost mali,

dixit ipse. quam fabellam tanto animi motu, tanta arte scripsit ut ipse inter classicos vivus insereretur, libro fatum Horatianum adsignaretur ut pueros elementa doceret.

Sed haec non diu circumvectari debemus. ille enim quem produco non est idem atque fabellae istius auctor. nam iudicibus tela intendentibus Proteus est mutabilis, ut scripsit,

> οὔτοι χελώνης δέρματ' ἀνδριὰς βλέπων.

itaque alio provectus est, thesauro morum et animi motuum studiosis relicto qualis vix in *Bacchis* Euripideis inest.

Quanta vi librum illum de apice ecclesiae summitati aptando composuit! columnas vi et pondere cantantes videmur audire, gaudii participes, opere ad maiorem Dei gloriam surgenti elati. sed qualibus haec fundamentis nituntur? nempe caeno, libidine, fraudatione, caede, morbo, superbia. Aeschylea haec digna sunt precatione:

> αἴλινον αἴλινον εἰπέ, τὸ δ' εὖ νικάτω.

Vis inest eadem in libro quem Περὶ διαβατηρίων nuper conscripsit, praemio illustri honestato; formam tamen et genus mutavit Proteus noster sagacissimus. auctoribus Anglicis maximis Oxoniae olim operam dedit: ecce nunc scriptorum valde Anglicorum auctor maximus.

Praesento vobis Gulielmum Golding, Excellentissimi Ordinis Britannici Commendatorem, Collegii Aenei Nasi honoris causa Socium, ut admittatur honoris causa ad gradum Doctoris in Litteris.

WILLIAM GOLDING
Writer

'THE deeds in which I shared', says Aeneas. He could equally have said 'the deeds which shared in me'. The writings of William Golding have the power of imparting deep feelings: past deeds become part of the reader, 'history felt in the blood and bones', and he shares in 'those moments which put a crown on life'. 'A little of Leonidas' is passed on to the reader and sticks in his mind.

He wrote *Lord of the Flies* because he was stirred by the malevolence latent in civilized men, which became all too apparent during the appalling war of 1939-45: 'man produces evil as a bee produces honey.' This myth was written with such art and such emotion that Golding became a classic in his own lifetime and the book achieved the fate which Horace foretold for his *Epistles:* it was prescribed for the A-level syllabus.

But we must not linger on this book. The man whom I present is not the same man as the author of *Lord of the Flies.* As he puts it, he is a 'moving target', not a statue which presents 'a po-faced image'; and so he has moved on, leaving a treasure-house for psychologists and anthropologists which may rival the *Bacchae.*

The Spire is written with great intensity. We hear the cathedral pillars singing under the strain, we share the Dean's joy, we are uplifted by the spire as it rises for the greater glory of God. But look at the foundations on which it rests: mud, lust, fraud, murder, disease, pride. Only Aeschylus can offer us an adequate reaction:

> Sing woe, woe, woe: but may the good prevail.

There is the same intensity in *Rites of Passage,* which won the Booker McConnell Prize in 1980, but our cunning Proteus has altered his form once again. Mr. William Golding once studied English Literature at Oxford: here now he is, an integral part of English Literature himself.

I present William Golding, CBE, Honorary Fellow of Brasenose College, for admission to the Honorary Degree of Doctor of Letters.

1983

IOHANNES BERTRAND GURDON

OVUM recens inseminatum quo modo in formam adultam mutatur? hoc iam dudum inquirit vir doctus quem produco, inquisivit olim post gradum Baccalaurei conlatum, cum Michaeli Fischberg discipulus consociatus, cuius in locum apud zoologos nostros postea successit. ovorum primum bufonis sive ranae collectorum nucleos, ut vocantur, exscidit. ovis deinde eisdem nucleos e cellulis quibusdam adultis abreptos insevit: ecce nucleorum tralatio! quid tum? tralati auxilium atque alimentum idoneum bufoni iam adulto suppeditare valuerunt; nimirum quia mandata quaedam quae in cellula qualibet insunt progressum eius gubernatura in cellis adultis integra conservantur latentque. hoc modo quaestionem hic solvit – paene dixeram *enucleavit* – a biologis iam inde ab aetate Aristotelis ipsius tentatam.

De mandatis eisdem quae *programmata* appellantur multa quae maximi momenti sunt indagavit. cum autem experimenta in cellulis vivis mallet facere quam in apparatu suo vitreo, cellulis moleculas multas et varias inserebat, miro quidem eventu. demonstravit enim cuniculi partem illam minimam quae haemoglobina creat munera propria posse exsequi ovo ranae insertam.

Societatis Regiae sodalis tunc ante annum quadragesimum electus Cantabrigiam decessit, quae biologis abundabat particularum genetricium scientissimis. illud praecipue ibi percontatus est quo modo particulae illae gubernentur, istaeque in primis quae πρωτείοις quibusdam arcessitis potestatem dant musculis se contrahendi.

Studia prima hic in Aede Christi exsecutus est, propter excellentiam quam in litteris humanioribus praestiterat adscriptus, ubi nuper in ordinem Studentium honoris causa electus est. oblectamenta autem habet quae laboribus suis biologis valde sunt consentanea: insectorum quae λεπιδόπτερα Graece vocantur peritus est, topiarius quoque est studiosus. o fortunatum cui licentia data est hortum proprium colendi! utinam felix sit ei ex arbusculis tralatio surculos diu serenti, inter papiliones laboranti.

Praesento vobis Iohannem Bertrand Gurdon, Societatis Regiae Sodalem, in Universitate Cantabrigiensi Professorem Collegiique Churchilliani Socium, ut admittatur honoris causa ad gradum Doctoris in Scientia.

JOHN BERTRAND GURDON
Biologist

HOW does a newly fertilized egg develop into a mature adult? This is the question which Professor John Gurdon has been studying for much of his life. He began his quest for an answer as a postgraduate student working with Mikhail Fischberg, whom he was later to succeed as John Wilfred Jenkinson Lecturer in the Department of Zoology here. In his first experiments he took eggs from a toad (he calls it a frog) and destroyed their nuclei. He then injected into those eggs nuclei taken from various adult cells, achieving thereby a nuclear transplant. And the result? He showed that the replacement nuclei were capable of supporting the development of an adult toad. He deduced that the information which programmes the development of an organism is retained in a latent form in each cell of an adult, and thereby answered (or should I say *enucleated*?) a problem which has been troubling biologists since Aristotle.

He has done a great deal of fundamental work on this system of programming. For his experiments he has preferred living cells to laboratory test-tubes, and his results have been remarkable. He has demonstrated, for instance, that the template which directs the synthesis of haemoglobin in rabbits can operate perfectly well if it is injected into the egg of a frog.

At that time, having been elected a Fellow of the Royal Society before the age of forty, he moved to Cambridge, which abounded with biologists who had detailed knowledge of genes. There the principal object of his research has been to analyse precisely how genes are controlled, concentrating especially on the genes which specify the important proteins which endow muscles with their ability to contract.

All his first work on biology was done here at Christ Church, where he was once admitted because of the excellence of his work in Classics, and where he is now an Honorary Student. His recreations are remarkably appropriate for a man whose main work is biology: he is interested in lepidoptera and is a keen gardener. Happy the man who can say, 'J'ai cultivé mon jardin.' I wish him many happy transplants, grafted from his shrubs, as he works amidst the butterflies.

I present John Gurdon, FRS, Fellow of Churchill College and John Humphrey Plummer Professor of Cell Biology in the University of Cambridge, for the Honorary Degree of Doctor of Science.

1988

BERNARDVS HAITINK

VIR adest qui mesochoros fere omnes praeclarissimos supereminet. in Batavis natus, a musicis Batavis doctus, iuvenis admodum mesochori in artibus praestitit. anno suo tricesimo tertio electus est qui collegium symphoniacorum Amstelodami in Odeo canentium moderaretur; mox symphoniacis etiam Londiniensibus qui φιλαρμονικοί vocantur praefectus est, musicorum deinde catervae illi praeclarae fabulas melicas ruri apud Saxones Australes agentium. neque tamen eo tempore munera sua Amstelodami suscepta remisit. curribus igitur aeriis ultro citroque quam celerrime totiens commeabat ut cum Batavo illo fabuloso qui adsidue volitabat haud inepte compararetur.

Volatus tamen non solum inter Anglos Batavosque sed etiam per orbem totum terrarum musicos moderandi causa saepe faciebat, ad Germanos, Helvetios, Russos, Americanos, Nipponenses, Argentinos ... sed *quo fessum rapitis?* tempus iam me deficit tot itinera enarrantem. ulterius etiam fama eius per gentes omnes pervolat,

εὐφώνων πτερύγεσσιν ἀερθεῖσ᾽ ἀγλααῖς Πιερίδων.

discis enim cereis opera plurima mandavit, in primis symphonias omnes Antoni Bruckner Gustavique Mahler, quorum nomina in nomismatibus duobus quibus honestatus est incisa reperietis.

Symphonias ita solet interpretari ut totam rationem operis facile comprehendant ei qui audiunt, critici modo artis aedificandi periti qui templi totius structuram partibus variis ex ordine descriptis dilucide exponit. modestia insignis est, vir ad agendum quam ad disserendum promptior, qui una cum symphoniacis suis paratus est ut *meditando* condiscat quid opus possit, quid in animo habuerit qui composuit. etenim totus est in laboribus musicis quos suscepit. in his desudat elaboratque, somni alimenti oblectationis incuriosus, proverbii nempe Ascraei memor:

τῆς δ᾽ ἀρετῆς ἱδρῶτα θεοὶ προπάροιθεν ἔθηκαν.

In fabulas praesertim melicas per lustra iam duo incumbit. nuperrime vero symphoniacis cantoribusque fabulas in Horto Monacharum Londiniensi canentibus praefectus est. opus hoc ei maximum scopulis mehercule refertum adgresso omnia bona fausta felicia fortunataque precamur.

Praesento vobis Bernardum Haitink, Musis amicum, honoribus praeclarissimis Batavorum Belgarum Francogallicorum cumulatum, Excellentissimi Ordinis Imperii Britannici Equitem honoris causa creatum, ut admittatur honoris causa ad gradum Doctoris in Musica.

BERNARD HAITINK
Conductor

AMONG distinguished conductors Bernard Haitink is pre-eminent. Born in the Netherlands and trained by Dutch musicians, he developed this excellence while he was still a young man. He was only thirty-two when he was appointed a Permanent Conductor of the Concertgebouw Orchestra of Amsterdam. A few years afterwards he became Principal Conductor of the London Philharmonic Orchestra, and later Musical Director at Glyndebourne. Throughout this period he retained his appointment in Amsterdam. He consequently commuted so frequently by air between Britain and the Netherlands that he was inevitably called 'The Flying Dutchman'.

He did not confine his flights to the London-Amsterdam service. He flew to conduct orchestras in Germany, Switzerland, Russia, North America, Japan, Argentina ... ; the full list is bewildering and would take too long to recite. But his fame has soared even further and is world-wide, 'raised high on the glorious wings of the melodious Muses', by virtue of the many records he has published, in particular his complete recordings of the symphonies of Bruckner and Mahler. He won the Bruckner Medal of Honour in 1970 and the Gold Medal of the International Gustav Mahler Society in 1971.

He interprets a symphony with such clarity that the audience can readily grasp the structure of the work. In this he resembles an architectural critic who by skilful and systematic analysis of the different parts of a temple can clearly bring out the structure of the building as a whole. He is notable among conductors for his moderation; he is happier doing things than talking about them, and he is willing to learn by *practice* along with his orchestra the potential of a score and what the composer had in mind. He becomes absorbed in his musical commitments: to these he devotes all his energy, oblivious of sleep, food, and recreation, for he knows full well the truth of Hesiod's maxim:

> In front of Excellence the gods put sweat.

For the past ten years Bernard Haitink has concentrated more on opera. Last September he was appointed Music Director of the Royal Opera House at Covent Garden. The task he has undertaken there is a great one and full of difficulties. We wish him all good fortune in his undertaking.

I present Bernard Haitink, musician, Hon. KBE, Chevalier de l'Ordre des Arts et des Lettres, who holds also the Orders of Orange Nassau and the Crown of Belgium, for the Honorary Degree of Doctor of Music.

1988

GVLIELMVS REDE HAWTHORNE

Caput nostrum tintinnat,
stridor ingravescit;
clangor ecce propinquat:
omnibus patescit.

QUANTO maiora cecinisset orator noster pristinus qui hos versus scripsit si ei contigisset *balaenae ballistariae* adesse cum viatoribus sescentis repleta ingenti vaporis ardentissimi impulsu praecipitata in aera conicitur!

Prodigiis tantis quid nunc est usitatius? quorum inter auctores hunc esse scitote quem nunc salutamus. machinas enim quibus propelluntur ab aliis inventas magnopere emendavit, qui rationem fluendi quam habeant res liquidae et ardentes indagavit, vaporum illorum calidorum egredientium morem et habitum mira sollertia excogitavit. itaque machinae potentiam maxime auxit, qua re machinis iam modicis tot viatores in caelum tolluntur.

Documentum hoc habemus clarissimum quid prosit coniunctio cum viris doctis Americanis. nam in Institutione technologiae transatlantica omnium Institutorum praestantissima professor electus studia haec sua protulit, quae deinde apud suos Cantabrigienses reversus perfecit.

Ibi per annos triginta studiis thermodynamicis praefuit. praefectus est etiam Collegio Churchilliano, Magister secundus electus, qui dignus visus est qui Iohanni Cockcroft succederet, quem olim nos honestavimus Oxonienses. hospes ibi est benignissimus, qui hospitia amplissima in nocturnas profert lucernas, dum de rebus maximi momenti trahuntur sermones, morem scilicet secutus herois eius Collegii eponymi. cuius post mortem epistulas collectas in Collegium Churchillianum curavit recipiendas digneque reponendas, donum quidem maxime idoneum. collegium autem habet optime contra temporum vices munitum, utpote qui diu in viribus naturalibus conservandis occupatus sit. ministerium quoque domesticis rebus praepositum consilio diu adiuvit ubi rerum naturalium scientia opus erat.

Accedat tandem studium huius inusitatum, ne gravitate tantae auctoritatis nimis onustum existimetis: artis magicae est peritus, rarissime post medium aevum in Universitatibus exercitae. qua arte nunc maxime egemus academici cum virorum talium experientia coniuncta ut Universitates et Collegia nostra salvis moribus, salva doctrina e temporum nostrorum angustiis evadant.

Praesento vobis Gulielmum Rede Hawthorne, Equitem Auratum, Excellentissimi Ordinis Britannici Commendatorem, Societatis Regiae Socium, Collegii Churchilliani apud Cantabrigienses Magistrum, ut admittatur honoris causa ad gradum Doctoris in Scientia.

SIR WILLIAM REDE HAWTHORNE
Engineer

What is this that roareth thus?
Can it be a Motor Bus?

MY predecessor A. D. Godley, who wrote these lines, would have been inspired to even greater efforts had he been privileged to be present at the take-off of a *Jumbo Jet* with hundreds of passengers.

Such marvels are now part of everyday life, and the honorand to whom we now pay tribute is to be reckoned one of the scientists principally responsible for them. For his work led to big changes in the existing jet engine. By his study of fluid flow and combustion he greatly improved our knowledge of the nature and behaviour of jet exhausts. He succeeded in increasing the power of the jet engine so that crowds of passengers can now be carried by engines of moderate size.

His career is a clear proof of the advantages of cooperation between British and American scientists. He did the bulk of this work as Professor at MIT and returned from Cambridge, Mass. to Cambridge, England to complete it.

At Cambridge he was Professor of Thermodynamics for thirty years. He is in addition Head of Churchill College, having been elected as an appropriate Master to succeed Sir John Cockcroft, also one of our honorands. At Churchill he is a superb host, prolonging his hospitality deep into the night while the conversation ranges over matters of great moment. In this he follows the tradition of the eponymous hero of Churchill College. The Churchill papers were an appropriate gift to the College, and as Master he received and housed them suitably. He keeps his College warm and well insulated, as befits a former Chairman of the Advisory Council on Energy Conservation. He has also devoted much time to the Home Office Scientific Advisory Council, and has been Chairman of that body too.

But his official duties have not made him too serious: he practises magic, an unusual pursuit and an art little cultivated in the Universities since the Middle Ages. It is an art which we now need in our Universities, in combination with the experience of men like the Master of Churchill, if we are to preserve our institutions in the present difficult times without damage to our traditions or the cause of Learning.

I present Sir William Hawthorne, CBE, FRS, Master of Churchill College, Cambridge, for admission to the Honorary Degree of Doctor of Science.

1982

DOROTHEA HODGKIN

ADEST quae Universitati nostrae Collegioque suo de Somerville ingentem famam ob praeclara reperta circumdedit. nam Iohanni Bernal Cantabrigiensi doctissimo adiutrix primo adscita novam chemiae gerendae artem extudit, de qua *paucis (adverte) docebo.*

Moleculas crystallinas percutiendas curavit radiis istis Roentgenianis quos metalla particulis electronicis eXcitata emittunt. itaque particulis his dissipatis primordiorum quae inerant ordo positura figura obscure discerni poterant. quorum compagem ut per coniecturam exacte definiret arte subtilissima atque ingenio maximo opus erat. tabulis enim multis quae res quasque depingebant altitudinem, ut ita dicam, et amplitudinem induere debebat. ratione hac nova moleculas rerum quarundam genti humanae utilissimarum recte descripsit, penicillini scilicet, insulini, elementi denique vitalis duodecimi. en Praxitelen cum Democrito coniunctum!

Rerum inventrix salutata honoribus multis cumulata est, praemio Nobeliano honestata, Universitatis Bristoliensis Cancellaria creata. muneribus tamen aliis semper vacat: discipulos docuit, virum liberosque tres fovit; libenter etiam Collegium novum de Linacre fundatum consilio adiuvit. perita enim fuit inter fremitum parvulorum orationesque sollemnes collegarum rite convocatarum operam curamque in rebus chemicis ponere.

Disciplina multos instituit qui chemia sunt praestantissimi. discipulam etiam quandam docuit chemicorum omnium nunc notissimam, civitatis nostrae principibus praefectam, quae artibus moleculas indagandi olim imbuta compagem iam totam rei publicae indagatam bene cognovit.

In Africa haec aliquando habitavit. colloquia quoque habet cum rerum inventoribus toto orbe divisis, Academiae Russorum Serumque adscripta. quid quaeris? praemio Leniniano ob pacem corroboratam donato nuper honestata est, nec non Praeses est Consilii rerum naturam indagantium ad vim primordiorum cohibendam instituti, cuius nomen vix Anglice, nedum Latine pronuntiare ausim. nonne licet huic iustissime

non sibi sed toti genitam se credere mundo?

Praesento vobis Dorotheam Hodgkin, Ordini insigniter Meritorum adscriptam, Societatis Regiae Sodalem, Professorem Emeritam, Collegiorum de Somerville deque Linacre honoris causa Sociam, ut admittatur honoris causa ad gradum Doctoris in Scientia.

DOROTHY HODGKIN
Crystallographer

PROFESSOR Dorothy Hodgkin's scientific discoveries have brought great distinction to our University and to her College, Somerville. She was the pioneer of a new technique in Chemistry, evolved after a period assisting the great J. D. Bernal in Cambridge.

Her method was to subject molecules of a crystalline substance to X-ray bombardment. From the resulting scattering of electrons the atomic structure of the molecule showed up indistinctly. The conjectural assembly of the molecule's skeleton required from her then the detailed skill of an artist. She had to work out a three-dimensional interpretation of an array of ordinary maps and pictures. By this new method she successfully discovered the atomic structure of the molecules of certain substances of great importance to mankind: penicillin, insulin, and vitamin B12. What a combination of arts! Here is both a sculptress and a physical scientist of the first order, Praxiteles united with Democritus.

After winning recognition for her discoveries she received many honours, including a Nobel Prize, and was elected Chancellor of Bristol University. Yet she always finds time for tasks unconnected with her research. She has taught pupils; she has cared for her husband and three children; she freely gave help and advice to a newly founded Oxford College, Linacre. Amid the clatter of children and the customary speeches of her colleagues at a College meeting she had the ability to concentrate on Chemistry.

Many of her pupils are eminent chemists. One in particular is now the most widely-known chemist of them all, since she holds the highest office in government. Trained in the art of analysing molecules, she has by now analysed and mastered the whole structure of the state.

Professor Hodgkin has lived for a time in Africa. She has meetings with distant scientists, as a Member of the Soviet and Chinese Academies. I may add that she has recently been awarded the Lenin Peace Prize and is President of PUGWASH, founded to monitor the use of atomic power. She has every right to believe that she was

> Born not for herself but for the world.

I present Dorothy Hodgkin, OM, FRS, Professor Emerita, Honorary Fellow of Somerville College and Linacre College, for the Honorary Degree of Doctor of Science.

1987

43

EMINENTISSIMVS CARDINALIS
BASILIVS HUME

PRIMUM salutamus Cardinalem Ecclesiae Catholicae et Romanae, Aulae Sancti
Benedicti alumnum. raro autem Cardinales post aetatem Thomae Wolsey
honoravimus. Arturum quidem Hinsley ad gradum doctoris honoris causa admisimus,
neque tamen audacia tunc abundavimus, gradus enim erat in Iure Civili. etenim venit in
mentem Cardinalis alius Oxoniensis imago, Iohannis Henrici Newman. o tempora iam
laetiora! o mores in melius mutatos! ab Universitate enim ille ob fidem debuit discedere,
diutissime non postea visurus: hunc maximo cum gaudio accipimus Oxonienses, nuper
in ecclesia Sanctae Mariae sacra praedicantem audivimus.

Abbas hic erat, abbatiae ordinis Sancti Benedicti remotae praeerat, de pueris
educandis curabat. subita illinc Pontificis Summi vocatione Archiepiscopus est electus,
Westmonasterium rure advectus, Cardinalis Romae creatus. lustro iam completo quanta
quot homines admiratione, sive fideles sive e partibus infidelium, sermones eius
audierunt, libros emerunt, effigiem vivam loquentis domi viderunt! popularis enim
electione illa factus est, cuius dicta omnia omnes in actis diurnis perscrutamur, sive
gravissimis *Temporum* vicibus commixta sive levissimis *Solis Vulgati* oblectamentis.
onerosum hoc viro qui monachus factus vitam legendi meditandique fortasse expecta-
verat, sed maxima data est ei facultas lucem in tenebris ferendi. neque desunt omnino
gaudia grammatici: vidi egomet palatium eius iuventute Londiniensi repletum,
Archiepiscopum ipsum κοινωνίᾳ μαλθακᾷ παίδων obsessum. vacat etiam interdum
Novocastrenses suos Coniunctos spectare pilam rotundam iactantes, gaudia ipsi pilae
ovatae experto.

Quanta hic et qualia iam perfecerit cognovistis. Archiepiscopus electus provinciae
administrandae modum totum commutavit, tempus sibi adscivit ad apostolatus
quosdam extra ordinem creatos, ad corpore deformatos iuvandos, ad iuventutem
fovendam, ad cives alienigenas civibus his nativis coniungendos. promptissimus est
ipse in agendo; raro frigore torpent filamenta telephonica quae domi instituit presbyteris
suis reservata: crebris vibrationibus calent, *calida* callide vocantur. conciliis permultis
praesidet, sanctis Romae conclavibus bis – ita Deo visum – Pontificem creavit,
colloquia sollemnia habet cum Episcopis Ecclesiae Anglicae Londiniensibus, consiliis
ut vocantur oecumenicis adest, qui non formulis verborum callidis sed altius
coniunctionem quaerendam esse credit.

Tria sunt quae provinciae suae commendavit: Preces, Fides, Actio. 'Nonne tribus
verbis omnis descripta patescit/ vita viri?' praesento vobis virum eminentissimum,
Basilium Hume, Cardinalem et Archiepiscopum, ut admittatur honoris causa ad gradum
Doctoris in Sacra Theologia.

CARDINAL BASIL HUME
Archbishop of Westminster

THE first honorand whom we salute is a Cardinal of the Catholic Church and a member of St. Benet's Hall. Oxford has very seldom honoured a cardinal since the days of Cardinal Wolsey. We gave an honorary degree to Cardinal Hinsley in 1942, but we then took care to avoid any rash action: his degree was in Civil Law, not Divinity. One cannot help thinking of another Oxonian Cardinal, John Henry Newman. The contrast points the happy change in the times: our attitudes have altered for the better. Newman had to leave this University when he changed his faith, and was not to see it again for a long time: whereas we joyfully welcome our guest here to the University of Oxford and we have recently heard him preaching in the University Church of St. Mary.

Our honorand was once an Abbot in charge of a Benedictine monastery and concerned with the education of schoolboys. Suddenly at the summons of the Pope he became Archbishop, he left the countryside for Westminster, and was created Cardinal at Rome. In his five years of office, millions of the faithful and millions of unbelievers have admired him, heard his addresses, bought his books and seen him on their television sets. That election had made him a public figure, whose pronouncements everybody reads whether in *The Times* or in *The Sun*: a burdensome task indeed for a man who on becoming a monk might have expected a life of reading and meditation, but a great opportunity for carrying light in dark places. He has not entirely lost the pleasures of schoolmastering: I have myself seen his palace crammed with the youth of London and the Archbishop in person besieged with 'the soft converse of children'. He also occasionally finds time to support Newcastle United, whose matches he can appreciate, having once himself experienced the joys of Rugby (wing-forward).

The number and quality of his achievements in five years is well known. When he became Archbishop he changed the whole administration of his diocese to give himself time for several special apostolates, for the disabled, for instance, for youth, and for racial harmony. He is a man of action; the special telephone line reserved for his diocesan priests is seldom inert: it hums and vibrates ceaselessly so that it is aptly called a 'hot line'. He presides over a great many committees and has twice (for such was the will of God) elected a Pope in conclave at Rome. He has regular meetings with the Anglican Bishops of the London dioceses and attends oecumenical councils. He does not believe in unity reached by the skilful manipulation of formulae; union, he feels, is a matter for deeper contemplation and search.

He has appointed three watchwords for his diocese: Prayer, Faith, Action. Is not the breadth and scope of his entire life revealed, as Horace put it, in these words?

I present his Eminence Basil Hume, Archbishop and Cardinal, for admission to the Honorary Degree of Doctor of Divinity.

1981

FREDERICVS HUMPHRIS

VIRUM produco qui per annos triginta duo geologos Oxonienses artificio adiuvit suo, qui una cum viris doctissimis strenue enisus est ut valeant 'pandere res alta terra caligine mersas'. officinae enim praepositus laboravit semper pro virili parte, si recte hoc dici potest de viro qui labores tam heroicos tentavit. nonne saxa durissima confregit hic quae vel Herculeae clavae restitissent? nonne fauces Tartareas ita invasit ut catenam longam maxima cura elaboratam demittendam curaret, qua ardores inferni certis modis cognoscerentur?

Haud ignota loquor; permulti enim vestrum imagines academicorum pervulgatas domi vidistis de novo saeculorum ordine qui iam nascitur docentium; itaque vobis bene notum esse credo *Herman Munster,* instrumentum scilicet ab hoc viro constructum, quo saxa διπλῆ μάστιγι percutiuntur, vi hac primum lacessita qua lux vicis domibusque nostris diffunditur, liquoris deinde compressi momento diffissa ingenti.

Illud tamen fortasse non est notum, instrumentum eum aliud fecisse cui nomen est insolitum *Evaporator,* quo vapores omnes qui in saxis latent eliciuntur, ne viris doctis obstent de aetate saxorum et ratione compositionis quaestionem facientibus. tertium iam instrumentum scholastica lege adiciam, apparatum nempe quem e cylindris duobus construxit, quorum alter recta semper via rotatur, alter autem dum rotatur exiguo clinamine, versibus Lucretianis dignissimo, interdum aberrat; inter quos rotatos depositum si saxum quoddam pertinacius esse videtur mox hoc tormento frangitur, arcana sua prodit.

Nolite tamen credere hunc totum esse in instrumentis: domum geologorum armariis cistisque decoris ornavit, cellas duas seiunctas et emundatas construxit Chemiae artibus dedicatas; thecas etiam fabricatus est ex omni latere patentes, in quibus exemplaria diversa e terra effossa manifesta potestis admirari.

Artificis talis non mirum est famam longe pervolitavisse. nuper autem nomine eius audito scholaris quidam Texanus, 'haud ignotum', dixit, 'memoras,' nam de hoc iam in Societate Americana Geologorum audiverat; 'nonne ille ὁ πάντεχνος?'

Praesento vobis Fredericum Humphris, virum τεχνικώτατον, optime de geologis nostris totaque scientia geologorum meritum, ut admittatur honoris causa ad gradum Magistri in Artibus.

FREDERICK HUMPHRIS
Instrument Maker and Designer

THE honorand whom I introduce has used his technical skill for the benefit of the Department of Geology for the past thirty-two years, working energetically with distinguished scientists

> to lay bare things
> Hid deep in earth and darkness.

Ever since he took charge of the Department's workshop he has laboured to do 'all that is humanly possible' to assist research – if indeed this is the right phrase for a man who has engaged in such heroic labours, breaking the toughest rocks, which would have resisted even the club of Heracles, and invading the Underworld with thermistor probes, inserted into the earth to measure terrestrial heat flux, by means of a cable-handling system which Mr. Humphris designed.

What I say is no news for many of you: if you watch programmes like 'Tomorrow's World' on the television you need no introduction to *Herman Munster,* the crushing machine invented by our honorand which subjects rocks to the 'double scourge' of electricity followed by hydraulic power.

But you may not know of another machine he has made, oddly called an *Outgasser,* which removes all the gas latent in a rock sample to prevent its getting in the way of experiments. And here is one more machine – to make a round three – consisting of two cylinders, one with a dead level rotation, the other rotating with a minute and irregular swerve, which would have appealed to Lucretius. Put between these rollers, a recalcitrant piece of rock is soon broken, yields to their torture, and gives up its secrets.

You must not, however, suppose that Mr. Humphris is totally engrossed in machines. He has equipped the Department of Geology with fine cases and cupboards of all kinds, and himself designed and constructed two ultra-clean chemical laboratories. He has also made showcases which give a very clear display of mineral specimens.

A craftsman like this naturally has a far-flung reputation. Only the other day a graduate student from Texas heard his name mentioned. 'Of course I know that name,' he said, for he had heard of Mr. Humphris at a meeting of the Geological Society of America. 'That's the man who can make *anything.'* I present Mr. Frederick Humphris, the most skilled of craftsmen, who has done excellent work for his Department here and for geological studies in general, for admission to the Honorary Degree of Master of Arts.

1981

ANDREAS HUXLEY

VIR adest de musculis sagacissimus. de musculis igitur canendum est quo modo contrahantur. 'haec ἀπόγραφα sunt: verba tantum adfero.'

> Musculus est duplex: subsunt duo fila petenti;
> huic myosini insunt vires, actina habet illud;
> hoc maius, minus est illud. nos membra movemus
> lubrica per filum filo labente superne
> seque modis miris intrinsecus insinuante.
> labitur en pedibus myosini particularum,
> quae caput erexere volubile continguntque
> particulas alias actini, quae subito iam
> vi myosini ictae coitus iunguntur amore;
> semper enim myosino actini pellicitur vis.

At enim talia notissima sunt, praecipit fortasse Orbilius, docent immo artis medicinae professores. ecce tamen cui praecipue haec debemus, vir dignus salutatione illa Vergiliana:

> felix qui potuit rerum cognoscere causas.

huic tamen curae sunt non solum causae sed etiam res ipsae. docuit enim de primordiis rerum medicos cognovisse debere qualia sint fila moleculaeque, neque tamen illa maiora esse ignoranda quae oculis manifesta sint vel vitro amplificata pateant.

Audite iam quaestiones quas nuper proposuit. num potest is de rerum conscientia satis dicere qui de coniuncta neuronum dispositione rationem dedit? si quid vivum est atque adultum cur laesum potest se redintegrare 'dum quod fuit ante reformet'? ad quaestiones has enucleandas sufficientne verba et rationes qualibus nunc utuntur rerum inventores? an deus ex machina est exspectandus qui nobis subveniat, qualis erat radii virium inventio vel rationis istius genetivae? o fortunatos rerum inventores quibus cursus studiorum inter certos terminos numquam haereat! nonne dixit ipse, 'vita taedio nulli datur'? ecce sententia vere Lucretiana, Societate Regia dignissima nec non gente universa Huxleia.

Praesento vobis Andream Huxley, Equitem Auratum, Societatis Regiae Praesidem, Praemio Nobeliano honestatum, Collegii Newtonensis honoris causa Socium, ut admittatur honoris causa ad gradum Doctoris in Scientia.

SIR ANDREW HUXLEY
Physiologist

S IR Andrew Huxley is a world expert on muscle. So here is a Latin poem about muscle and the way it contracts. 'It is all derivative', coming mainly from his Sherrington Lectures for 1976/7.

> Muscle contains two types of filament, one larger and composed of myosin, one smaller and composed of actin. Men move freely by means of muscle contraction, which occurs when the large filaments slide over and in between the smaller ones. They slide on 'micro-legs', composed of myosin molecules whose heads swivel as they touch actin molecules, which react to the myosin and link with it, since actin is responsive to the attraction of myosin.

You may smile, for this explanation is now something that every schoolboy knows, or at any rate every medical student. Here is the man to whom primarily we owe this knowledge, who indeed deserves to be saluted in the words Virgil applied to the scientific philosopher:

> Happy the man who can find out the causes of things.

But Professor Huxley is interested in the 'things' as well as the 'causes'. He has shown us that while the physiologist must be aware of fundamental constituents at the level of filaments and molecules he must not neglect observations at a higher level, of things which may be seen by the eye or with a microscope.

In his Romanes Lecture (1983) he has raised large questions for speculation. How far is it possible to give an account of human consciousness in terms of the complex system of neuronal circuits in the brain? Why has an adult organism the power to recover and 'resume its former shape' after an injury? Are these problems which will be solved in current scientific terms? Or are we waiting like the audience in the Theatre of Dionysus for some *deus ex machina* – such as the discovery of radioactivity or the genetic code – to come to our assistance? O happy scientists whose work is so unpredictable! 'Our lives are not dull,' his lecture concludes. Here is a statement reminiscent of Lucretius, poet and scientist, and worthy of the Royal Society and the whole Huxley family.

I present Sir Andrew Huxley, President of the Royal Society, Nobel Prizewinner, and Honorary Fellow of Trinity College, Cambridge, the College of Newton, for admission to the Honorary Degree of Doctor of Science.

1983

ROMANVS JAKOBSON

ΗΕΛΙΟΝ λέσχη κατεδύσαμεν: ita poeta Graecus cum amico modicum tempus terebat. amplius poeta recentior Mayakovsky, qui de amico iucundo cecinit qui per noctem totam de Romano Jakobson colloquium fecerat. ego quoque laudibus eius libenter diem hunc totum consumere velim, 'noctem addens operi'. fata tamen obstant; academicos iam audio mussantes, 'unde / ingenium par materiae?' temptandum igitur si dignum quid praeconio brevi valeam complecti.

Mirum habet hic carminum amorem, magnam de carminibus sollertiam, epicis praecipue vetustis Slavonicis. nonne carmen illud antiquum de Igore Principe, ab alienigena lacessitum tamquam a recentioribus confectum, strenue hic pro medio aevo vindicavit? etenim sacram illam linguam Slavonicam a Sancto Cyrillo Sanctoque Methodio usurpatam ita tractavit ut momentum atque adeo initium hoc esse demonstraret populorum aliquorum in Europa nostra in nationem coeuntium.

Studiorum etiam linguisticorum fundamenta aedificavit. professor enim Universitatis Caroleae electus Pragensem circulum (recte solet ita dici, ipse demonstravit) cum aliis instituit. quid memorem χαρακτῆρας illos in linguis *distinctos* quos ille circulusque suus petebant, alibi inter se consentientes, alibi repugnantes, regulas illas linguisticas omnibus ubique linguis communes quas invenit? o laborem Herculeum! *nec vero Alcides tantum telluris obivit.* in primis erat ille linguisticorum qui aphasiam investigabant, rem prius medicis reservatam. multa etiam de facultate verba discendi necnon dediscendi invenit. perlegant curiosi quod scripsit de verbis puerilibus 'matrem' et 'patrem' significantibus: nonnulla horum consonantem naso proditam continere: talem esse maiorem partem verborum 'matrem' significantium, partem tamen multo minorem 'patrem' significantium, neque mirum hoc esse; signum enim naso proditum proprium esse infantibus ad m-m-mammam matris lactantem occupatis.

Bene hic cognovit studia linguistica partem esse studiorum σημειωτικῶν ut nunc vocantur, multaque cum studiosis anthropologiae, zoologiae, sociologiae colloquitur. vacat tamen poemata auctorum recentiorum, quales sunt Blake, Baudelaire, Yeats excutere, atque rationes conscribendi invenire quas si cognoscerent quanta admiratione stuperent inscii auctores ipsi! solet hic Terentianum illud dicere: 'linguista sum: linguistici nihil a me alienum puto.' καὶ μεταποίησον, Λιγυαστάδη, ὧδε δ' ἄειδε: '*nihil* a me alienum puto.'

Praesento vobis Romanum Jakobson, multis multarum nationum honoribus cumulatum, quinque iam libris ingentibus honorificis ornatum, ut admittatur honoris causa ad gradum Doctoris in Litteris.

ROMAN JAKOBSON
Linguist

> … how often you and I
> Had tired the sun with talking and sent him down the sky.

WE all know how Callimachus spent his evenings. Mayakovsky had more time to spare, for he recalls in his verse the pleasures of conversing with his friend Nette who 'talked all night of Roman Jakobson'. I too would gladly spend all day on this topic and 'add night to the task'. But it cannot be; I already hear members of Congregation muttering, 'Too much material for one man to tackle'. So I must do my best to say something brief and suitable about Professor Jakobson.

Our guest has a wonderful affection and feeling for poetry, above all medieval Slavonic epics. When a foreigner attacked the venerable 'Igor' epic claiming that it was a modern concoction, it was Jakobson who vigorously defended it as medieval and authentic. Similarly he has treated Old Church Slavonic, that holy language used by St Cyril and St Methodius, and shown that this language provided an impetus, and indeed a beginning, for the movement to national self-determination of which we have seen much in Europe.

He has also laid the foundations of modern linguistics. As Professor at the Charles University he was a co-founder of the Prague Circle ('circle' is a proper metaphor used by linguists, as he has demonstrated). The concept of 'distinctive features' in languages which he and his circle strove to determine is most important – some such features co-existing in a language while others are mutually exclusive; he has in fact established a set of universal rules common to all languages. This was a labour of Hercules, and indeed covers more ground than even Hercules traversed. He was among the first linguists to investigate aphasia, a phenomenon previously left to the doctors. He has also made many discoveries about the faculty of learning (and forgetting). The curious should read his article, 'Why Mama and Papa?' The majority (55%) of the words meaning 'mother' contain a nasal consonant, but far fewer (15%) of the words meaning 'father'; and no wonder: for a nasal is appropriate to children sucking their m-m-mother's breast for they are too preoccupied to make any other noise.

Roman Jakobson is well aware that linguistic studies are a part of 'semiotics' and he has had much discussion with anthropologists, zoologists, and sociologists. Yet he has found time to analyse in detail some poems by recent authors like Blake, Baudelaire, and Yeats, and discover principles of composition which would have amazed their innocent authors. He is wont to apply Terence's *dictum* to himself: 'I am a student of language: I regard nothing which has to do with language as foreign to me.' Let me correct him in words once used by Solon: 'Just make one change, clear singer, and sing it thus instead: "I regard *nothing* as foreign to me."'

I present Roman Jakobson, who has received many honours in many countries, and has already been presented with five massive volumes of *Festschriften*, for admission to the Honorary Degree of Doctor of Letters.

1981

ROY JENKINS

TUAS nunc, Illustrissime, accingar dicere laudes; vos iam, egregii Procuratores, adloquor. Cancellario hoc creato maxime gaudent viri docti quibus mos maiorum placet, qui eadem rite repetita amant. ecce succedit Balliolensis Balliolensi; Doctor in Iure Civili vi ac virtute Diplomatis fit qui ad gradum Doctoris in Iure Civili honoris causa quondam admissus est; Cancellarius iterum est qui Cancellarius alibi quondam fuit, aerario scilicet praefectus.

Ab examinatoribus nostris olim probatus summa cum laude discessit. quo tempore licuit ei studia inter nos exercere,

> atque inter silvas Academi quaerere verum.

neque a vita hac academica omnino refugit. quamvis enim negotiis maximis occupatus, studia tamen multa perfecit, libros multos inter senatorum strepitus clamoresque populi docte atque eleganter composuit. quorum aliis alii magis placent; mihi quidem elegantissime de isto principe civitatis videtur scripsisse qui viris nostris nobilissimis in domum venerabilem convocatis tamquam deliciis suis ad nutum suum usque pipiantibus usus esse dicitur.

Ad rem publicam capessendam simul incubuit. etenim cum res penes partes operariorum essent officiis amplissimis summa cum dignitate, auctoritate summa functus est, multa correxit atque emendavit, clementiam magnam praestitit. postea cum collegis tribus ita a partibus istis descivit ut novas crearet, quarum Praeses primus ipse fuit, quis, quaeso, nescit de grege illo coniuratorum, ut vocantur, quattuor? ecce triumviratus praepotens femina adscripta quadratus.

Hactenus de rebus domi gestis dixi. plurima autem sunt quae foris adsecutus est. gentes enim Europaeas conglutinandi iamdudum studiosus, concilio summo gentium Europaearum per sex annos praefuit, nec non praemio nomine Caroli Magni insignissimo merito honestatus est. itaque quem virum doctum olim esse cognoveramus, *vir Europaeus* idem nunc salutandus est. nonne id meruit quod poeta ille antiquus dulcissimum esse dixit:

> πρᾶγμα δὲ τερπνότατον τοῦ τις ἐρᾷ τὸ τυχεῖν?

enixe huic laboranti plurima profluenter et prospere cesserunt: Cancellario nunc Universitatis Oxoniensis instituto omnia bona fausta felicia fortunataque precamur.

LORD JENKINS
Chancellor and Politician

NOW I must gird myself to sing your praises, Sir, and I address myself to the Proctors. Our recent choice of a Chancellor has great attractions for those Senior Members who are traditionalists, who like to see history repeating itself in due order. Here is a Balliol man succeeding a Balliol man; a new Doctor of Civil Law by Diploma who was in 1973 admitted to the honorary degree of Doctor of Civil Law; a Chancellor who has already been Chancellor in another place, in charge of the Exchequer.

After winning a First Class in Schools Mr Roy Jenkins could have entered on an academic career,

> In cloistered colleges to seek the truth.

He did not totally reject academic life. Despite the great pressure of important business he has completed much scholarly work. Undeterred by the buzz of Parliamentary life and the strident voices of the public, he has written many fine books. Every reader has his own favourite; mine is *Mr. Balfour's Poodle.*

At the same time he has plunged fully into public life. In Labour governments he held high office with distinction. As Chancellor of the Exchequer and Home Secretary he initiated many reforms and acted with great clemency. Subsequently with three colleagues he left Labour to create a new political party, and was its first President. The 'Gang of Four' is famous; here was a powerful triumvirate, made four-square by a woman member.

These are all achievements at home, here in Britain. His work abroad has also been fruitful. He has always striven hard for European unity. We greet him now as a former President of the European Commission, who has been deservedly honoured with the Charlemagne Prize. The *vir doctus* we once knew must be saluted as *vir Europaeus.* By his hard work he has earned what Theognis calls,

> Sweetest of all, to win the heart's desire.

His labours in public life have been crowned with great success; on his installation as Chancellor I use the traditional formula to wish him good luck: *omnia bona fausta felicia fortunataque precamur.*

1987

KIRI TE KANAWA

ADESTE tandem Patris Omnipotentis Angeli excelsiores: ordinem iam arcesso Seraphim clarissimorum, ut superne adsistentes inter imagines has depictas Veritatis triumphantis voltu ardente et fausto intueamini. requiem enim vos olim Samson dedistis hostibus turbulente eversis perculso. nunc hora adest postrema cum haec est salutanda quae nuper voce ipsa vos angelica arcessivit post diuturna sollemnia nuptiarum regalium ut Principi nostro et coniugi tranquillitatem daretis.

Londinium haec a Nova Zelandia prima iuventute advecta voci excolendae operam dedit, in terris etiam permultis cantavit, quae partes maximas in fabellis musicis egit, Toscae, Violettae, Annae Bolenae, Didonis, Arabellae, Tatianae – Elvirae in primis amore perditissimo percussae; ecce vocis dulcedo suavissima cum libidine flagrantissima coniuncta. gaudet enim ipsa cantando, gaudent qui adsunt gaudenti; inest vis et hilaritas quaedam rivulo similis qui solet 'plano scatere atque erumpere campo'; quae tum potentissimae sunt cum partibus idoneis coniunctae sunt. lacteam eius ubertatem audite Desdemonae ultima ista et tristissima carmina cantantis vel verba Paminae perturbatione vexatae, quibus

$$\text{ἀνδρῶν ἰφθίμων λύτο γούνατα καὶ φίλον ἦτορ.}$$

verba repeto censoris *Temporum* consideratissimi.

Neque genti tantum rariori quae fabellas tales audire solet nota est. fama enim eius ad populum totum pertinet. cui cum primum e patria et gente Maoriana discedendum fuit, quota pars populi istius carmen illud quod Maoris viaticum sive προπεμπτικόν est cantantem eam audivit, verba modosque quanto animi motu repetivit! etenim nuper cum angelos illos arcessebat vacua tunc erant strata viarum, nam domi vocem eius audiebant fere omnes Britannici.

Praesento vobis Kiri Te Kanawa, Excellentissimi Ordinis Imperii Britannici Dominam Commendatricem, Collegii de Somerville honoris causa Sociam, ut admittatur honoris causa ad gradum Doctoris in Musica.

DAME KIRI TE KANAWA
Singer

'LET the bright Seraphim in burning row' attend our Congregation. Come to assist us, standing on high among these paintings of Truth Triumphant and look upon us favourably with burning gaze. To Samson once you gave rest after his turbulent overthrow of his foes. Now is the hour when we must salute Kiri Te Kanawa, who called you but lately with her own angelic voice at the end of the long ceremonies of our Royal Wedding to grant a happy issue to our Prince and his Bride.

Kiri Te Kanawa left New Zealand as a young woman and came to London to train her voice. She has performed in many countries and has sung all the great operatic parts, Tosca, Violetta, Anna Bolena, Dido, Arabella, Tatiana – above all, Donna Elvira in the grip of desperate love; a wonderful combination of vocal sweetness and burning passion. Her enjoyment in her singing is infectious. She has a forceful, effervescent personality which when harnessed to a strong operatic part is very powerful. Listen to the creaminess of her voice as she sings Desdemona's tragic last songs, or the part of Pamina, anxious and distressed, which

'turns grown men's knees to jelly';

I quote the scholarly critic of *The Times*.

Her reputation is not confined to those who regularly go to hear operas. Her fame has spread to the whole population at large. When she had to leave her home in New Zealand and her fellow Maoris, a remarkable number of the people there heard her singing the Maori song of farewell and reiterated the words and music with deep emotion. Indeed when she summoned the bright Seraphim to London the streets here were empty, for nearly all the inhabitants of Britain were at home listening to her singing.

I present Dame Kiri Te Kanawa, DBE, Honorary Fellow of Somerville College, for admission to the Honorary Degree of Doctor of Music.

1983

PHILIPPVS LARKIN

Ἐν πολυτρόποις συμφοραῖς ἐπίστασθε τραφέντες. casibus his si quis moribus antiquis etiam laetatur magis in dies offenditur. aetas enim advenit effrenandae licentiae,

mi tamen ipsi
languidus ecce vigor neque in hos servatus amores.

verba cum dolore aliquo repeto quae cecinit hic qui adest persona senioris indignantis adhibita. quicquid iam deis supplicationis venerationisve proferimus, nostri saeculi non est nisi palam et in conventu plurium praestare:

Decessere Numae divum secreta colentes
numina, nunc etiam deficit ipse Deus.

quid autem collega isto molestius qui gravissima viris doctis praelocuturus peregrinatus est patriae solemnia sacra irridens?

Cum patribus populoque penatibus et magnis dis
principibus cramben placuit repetisse molestam.

bibliothecarius hic est qui versus limate scribit – quis nisi Callimachus? – rustici tamen cuiusdam *more legendi* adfectus est qui libros ineptiis insulsis refertos perlegerat dum stimulos malesuados et libidines petit, libros tandem omnes frustra abiecit.

Obscena haec neque praetermittit neque flagello Iuvenalis more castigat: exponit tantum placide, monitis obtemperans poetae nostri:

Lumina per casus vitae mortisque severa
flecte locoque citis cede, viator, equis.

neque tamen in sapientium illa templa serena recessit, qui dum iter facit novas nuptas cum comitatu obvias oblatas atque loca omnibus bene nota tam accurate depinxerit. carmina autem Stoicos veteres aliquando olent; etenim si accuratius legetis admonitus aliquid certi invenietis, dum senatoris uxorisque effigies antiquas ab eo iussi intuemini:

nil nisi noster amor nobis valet esse superstes.

Cum universitate nostra consociatus est ex quo tirocinio hic functus est iuveni illi similis – vel potius dissimilis – quem in novella depinxit. socius etiam Collegii Omnium Animarum electus dignus visus est qui poetarum huius aetatis florilegium componeret. invidiosum hoc opus aequales tamquam classicos notandi atque adeo laboriosum. noluit enim e florilegiis aliorum carmina excerpere, τἀλλότριον ἀμῶν θέρος. in sedibus igitur infernis bibliothecae Bodleianae carmina recentiora diu perlegit. o laborem scelestorum poenis simillimum! multa quoque de eo genere musicae cuius studiosus est scripsit; nuper etiam edidit *Maecenatum iussa,* libellos scilicet quosdam collectos, praemio insigni honestatos.

Praesento vobis Philippum Larkin, Excellentissimi Ordinis Imperii Britannici Commendatorem, Collegii Divi Iohannis Baptistae honoris causa Socium, honoribus permultis cumulatum, ut admittatur honoris causa ad gradum Doctoris in Litteris.

PHILIP LARKIN
Poet

YOU know (as Pericles put it) that you have been reared in an age of startling vicissitudes, which have delivered successive shocks to the traditionalist. An age of moral laxity has arrived

> rather late for me,

if I may echo Mr Larkin's sardonic words. Religion must now be social: we have no room for the hermit

> Talking to God (who's gone too).

Our honorand has evidently suffered from the peripatetic academic colleague who flies abroad to deliver lectures of great significance, sneering at the Remembrance Day service in London:

> That day when Queen and Minister
> And Band of Guards and all
> Still act their solemn-sinister
> Wreath-rubbish in Whitehall.

Here is a University Librarian who writes polished verses – a twentieth-century Callimachus – and is yet concerned with the 'reading habits' of a lout who has read rubbish for kicks and abandoned it.

Mr Larkin does not ignore these shocking phenomena, nor does he castigate them with the scourge of a satirist. He describes them in the detached language of one who has obeyed Yeats' final injunction:

> Cast a cold eye
> On life, on death,
> Horseman, pass by.

Yet he does not retreat into an academic ivory tower, for in *The Whitsun Weddings* he describes with loving care the people he meets on a journey, the brides and their families, and the everyday view from the train. One is sometimes reminded of the ancient Stoic writers; and indeed the reader who looks finds some hints of a positive attitude, as when he is invited to contemplate the stone effigies of the nobleman and his lady:

> What will survive of us is love.

His long connection with Oxford goes back to the time when he served his apprenticeship here as a freshman, like (perhaps rather *unlike*) the hero of his novel *Jill*. He has been a Visiting Fellow of All Souls, and was asked to edit a successor to the *Oxford Book of Modern Verse*. It is a stern and invidious task to construct a canon of one's contemporaries. Scorning to reap 'other men's flowers' from other anthologies, he lived laborious days in the nether regions of the Bodleian Library reading recently published poems – an occupation reminiscent of the punishment of the Great Sinners. He has written a great deal about jazz, and has recently published a collection of essays, *Required Writing,* which won the W. H. Smith Literary Award for 1983.

I present Philip Larkin, CBE, Honorary Fellow of St John's College, who has won numerous awards and prizes (Coventry Award of Merit 1978, Queen's Gold Medal for Poetry 1965, Loines Award for Poetry 1974, A. C. Benson Silver Medal RSL 1975, Foreign Honorary Member of the American Academy of Arts and Sciences) for admission to the Honorary Degree of Doctor of Letters.

1984

FREDERICVS MANN

AGMEN hoc doctorum ducit legum interpres ingeniosissimus, quem tibi virum vere Europaeum, Illustrissime, licet agnoscere. nam in Germania natus, apud Germanos Helvetios Anglos educatus, Londinium tandem patriae tempore iniquissimo advenit; in Universitate Bonnensi Professor est honoris causa; Concilium Europae adiuvit; apud iudices qui inter civitates Hagae Comitum iudicant causas nonnullas dixit, causam praecipue civitatis Belgicae notissimam. concilio insuper ad leges Germanorum foeda dominatione depravatas corrigendas instituto adscitus est.

Recte virum talem κόσμου πολίτην salutamus. moribus tamen Anglicis maxime imbutus est, quippe qui Londini officia iuris consulti per quadraginta tres annos exsequatur, iuris etiam nostri quod *commune* vocatur defensor exstiterit cum legibus novis Europaeis promulgatis detrimentum id accepturum esse censuerit, concilio praeterea ab Excelso Domino Cancellario ad leges nostras recensendas emendandasque fundato auxilium saepe attulerit.

De rebus pecuniariis quae ab iuris consultis tractantur et disputantur opus conscripsit *magnum, Iuppiter, et laboriosum*, quod auctoritate tanta est compositum ut quater iam per dimidiam partem saeculi repetitum 'enchiridion' apte vocetur cum in manibus etiam nunc sit omnium qui de iure consulentibus respondent. leges praeterea atque iura quae inter gentes omnes sancta servantur, quorum est peritissimus, accuratissime perscrutatus est.

De iudicum arbitriis iudex ipse est severus. nempe iudicem quendam primi ordinis a via recta sine causa sine ratione ultro aberravisse nuper scripsit; necnon pari usus simplicitate res ab aliis eiusdem ordinis diiudicatas hoc modo castigat:

> non potest fieri quin id colligamus, iudices illos celsissimos sententias quasdam sponte sua ultro dixisse quibus fundamenta solida rerum certarum et definitarum omnino defuerint, quarumque fons et origo prorsus fuerit inexplicabilis.

Octagenarius iam indole praeditus est vegetissima. bene quidem in exordio enchiridii sui maximi verba haec Plinii repetivit, epistularum scriptoris impigerrimi:

> studeamus igitur nec desidiae nostrae praetendamus alienam. sunt qui audiant, sunt qui legant; nos modo dignum aliquid auribus, dignum chartis elaboremus.

etenim ipse libros nonnullos signo Preli Oxoniensis distinctos edidit, libellos complures doctissimos scripsit, praelectionibus academicos – experto mihi credite – delectavit. merito igitur praelectiones anniversarias nomine eius insignes instituerunt collegae Londonienses, quas iam pronuntiaverunt viri doctissimi, in primis Vicecancellarius noster insignissimus, nec non Baro ille praeclarus de Hailsham quem Dominum Cancellarium quondam salutavimus.

Nonne ergo virorum doctorum huic gregi debet adscribi? at enim gregis alterius est, iuris scilicet consultorum oratorumque qui in foro cottidie versantur. nempe δαίμονι illi Platonico similis est qui deos hominesque conciliat, quippe qui interpretetur θεοῖς τὰ παρ' ἀνθρώπων καὶ ἀνθρώποις τὰ παρὰ θεῶν. qua in comparatione disne academicos similes esse censeo an hominibus? tantum in medio relinquam, *adhuc sub iudice lis sit*.

Praesento vobis Franciscum Fredericum Mann, Excellentissimi Ordinis Imperii Britannici Commendatorem, Academiae Britannicae Sodalem, apud Bonnenses honoris causa Professorem, Doctorem iam in Universitatibus duabus, ut admittatur honoris causa Doctoris in Iure Civili.

FREDERICK MANN

European Jurist

THIS learned procession is headed by a lawyer of great brilliance, whom you may, Mr
Chancellor, recognize as a true European. He is a German by birth, educated in Germany,
Switzerland, and England, who emigrated eventually to London during the troubled times of
the thirties. He is an Honorary Professor of the University of Bonn; he assisted the Council of
Europe; and he has on occasion acted as counsel at the International Court of Justice at the
Hague, where he represented the Belgian Government in a well-known case. After the war he
was a member of a committee for the denazification of German law.

Such a man may properly be reckoned a citizen of the world. Yet Dr Mann is thoroughly
versed in English ways and customs. Since 1946 he has been practising as a solicitor in London.
He came forward as a champion of our Common Law when he took the view that it would be
harmed by the development of a new body of European law. He has also served on numerous
working parties of the Law Commission, which reviews and reforms the laws of this country.

His book *The Legal Aspect of Money* is what Catullus called Heaven to witness as 'a big book
packed with work'. Four times edited in the last half-century, it is a manual in the true sense of
the word, in the hands of all legal consultants. In his other publications Dr Mann has devoted
much care and attention to questions of international law, in which he is an expert.

His own judgment of judgments made by the courts is stern. He has recently written of a
Law Lord that 'wholly inexplicably and wholly unjustifiably' he 'for the first time took the
wrong turn'. He uses equally plain language in criticizing the decision of other Law Lords: 'The
inexorable conclusion must be that ... the House independently made findings which lacked
any foundation in fact and the origin of which defies explanation.' He is a most active
octogenarian. In the preface to his great manual he quotes these appropriate words of Pliny,
that indefatigable letter-writer: 'So let us pursue our studies rather than make the idleness of
others the pretext for our own. There are always those who listen and those who read. It is for
us to labour towards what is worth being heard or printed.'

He has himself published several books with the Clarendon Press, he has written many
learned articles, and his lectures have delighted academic audiences (here I speak from experience). Thus the honour of a series of annual lectures named after him, established by his
colleagues in the firm of Herbert Smith and Co., is well deserved. These have been delivered by
lecturers of the highest calibre, notably our own Vice-Chancellor and the former Lord
Chancellor, Lord Hailsham.

Should he not therefore be classed as an academic, one of the throng so well represented
here? Yet he belongs to another throng, those lawyers who practise daily in the law courts. He
is really like Plato's δαίμων, that spirit who reconciles gods and men by interpreting 'to the gods
what men are saying and to men what the gods are saying'. Am I here comparing academics to
gods or men? I leave this question open; let it remain *sub judice*.

I present Francis Frederick Mann, CBE, FBA, Honorary Professor of Law in the University
of Bonn, Doctor in the Universities of Berlin and London, for the Honorary Degree of
Doctor of Civil Law.

1989

IRIS MURDOCH

DUBLINENSEM produco, Collegii de Somerville alumnam, quae litteras humaniores doctissime excoluit. nonne colloquio illo paene fabuloso interfuit quod de fabula Aeschylea *Agamemnone* a viro eruditissimo Eduardo Fraenkel diu habitum est? quae studia cum litterarum Anglicarum studiis felicissime coniunxit, academico praeclaro Oxoniensi nupta. annos fere quindecim in Collegio Sanctae Annae philosophiae studiosas docuit, postea ad libros scribendos totam se contulit.

In scriptis philosophicis ἀνομίαν magnam in doctrinis huius aetatis ethicis castigavit. Platonica enim est aperte, mysteriis Platonicis imbuta, quae sermones duos Socraticos nuperrime composuit. verbis autem usa philosophorum nostrorum librum Platone dignum de auctoritate et imperio Boni conscripsit. nam censet Boni ipsius formam seu speciem, a Platone αὐτὸ τὸ ἀγαθόν appellatam, vim maximam habere; exemplar hoc Boni homines exemplis bonorum doctos intueri, quod lumine suo veram omnium rerum naturam illustret.

Fabellas etiam permultas scripsit quas ad philosophiam ipsius vix pro certo attinere adfirmaverim, licet grammatici certent. in hoc quoque genere scribendi ἀνομίας castigatrix exstitit, illius scilicet qua scriptores hos qui nunc sunt in moribus fingendis vitiatos esse dixit. personas autem quas ipsa inducit *sine ira et studio* depingit, non tamen sine misericordia quadam et humanitate. locorum et morum proprietates accurate notat; quas acutissimo fortasse stilo repraesentat in libro illo subtili componendo cui titulus est Θάλαττα Θάλαττα, praemio insigni honorato, vel in collegio quodam Christiano describendo quod in fabella de tintinnabulo scripta finxit: inter piam et sollemnem Dei reverentiam quot motibus tument animi, quantis libidinibus! quanta mali conscientia tamquam Furiis agitantur isti sodales!

μύθῳ nempe maxime pollet, quae res ita explicat ut lectorem semper exspectatione suspendat. qua subtilitate eam nos saepe in futuro delectaturam esse speramus.

Mulierem praesento quae cum gravitatem Socratis tum Petronii delicias lectoribus praestitit, Irim Murdoch, Excellentissimi Ordinis Imperii Britannici Dominam Commendatricem, Collegiorum de Somerville et Sanctae Annae nec non Collegii Sancti Antonii Sociam honoris causa, ut admittatur honoris causa ad gradum Doctoris in Litteris.

DAME IRIS MURDOCH
Writer

DAME Iris Murdoch was born in Dublin. She showed great scholarly talent when she read for Greats in Somerville College, and was a member of Professor Eduard Fraenkel's learned and legendary seminar on the *Agamemnon*. Her work in *Litterae Humaniores* was most happily linked with English studies when she married a distinguished English scholar, John Bayley. For some fifteen years she taught the St Anne's philosophers, and then decided to devote herself entirely to writing.

As a philosopher she stands out in opposition to the laxity of modern ethics. She is an avowed Platonist, steeped in the mysteries of Plato's teaching, and has recently composed two Socratic dialogues. In her Platonic treatise *The Sovereignty of Good,* written in the language of modern philosophy, she argues that the Idea of Good, Plato's αὐτὸ τὸ ἀγαθόν, has dynamic power. Men learn from examples of good men to have a sight, or intuition, of the Form or Exemplar of Good, 'as the source of light which reveals to us all things as they really are'.

Her novels are not immediately and unquestionably linked with her philosophy; critics may argue about a connection. In this *genre* also she takes a stand against laxity, criticizing the lack of cohesion in the characterization of modern novelists. She presents her own subjects with detachment, but also with some sympathy. Their characters and the atmosphere of the places where they live are depicted with great care – most acutely, perhaps, in *The Sea, The Sea,* which won the Booker Prize, or in the representation of the Christian community in *The Bell*: in a setting of piety and worship what passions and lusts are stirring, what guilty consciences the members of the community have to torment them, as potent as the Furies of old.

Her plots are particularly strong: she always keeps her reader in suspense. We all hope that she will long continue to give us pleasure with fresh plots.

Here is an honorand who has offered her readers both the seriousness of Socrates and the delights of Petronius. I present Dame Iris Murdoch, DBE, Honorary Fellow of Somerville College, St Anne's College, and St Antony's College, for the Honorary Degree of Doctor of Letters.

1987

IAPONIAE PRINCEPS REGALIS
CELSISSIMVS NARUHITO

CANCELLARIVS MAGISTRI SCHOLARES
VNIVERSITATIS OXONIENSIS
OMNIBVS AD QVOS PRAESENTES
LITTERAE PERVENERINT
SALVTEM IN DOMINO SEMPITERNAM

CVM diu ex more nobis fuerit civitatum externarum illustrissimos Imperatores Reges Principes honorare, eosque praesertim qui propter doctrinam moresque spectatos inclaruerint:

CVMQVE Iaponiae Princeps Regalis Celsissimus NARUHITO rerum academicarum sit peritissimus nec non ruris nostri Oxoniensis, quippe qui a Professoribus suis Nipponensibus primo eruditus studia postea Oxoniae exercuerit, de proavis nostris fluvium hunc Tamesim lintribus onerariis navigantibus librum magnum atque doctum conscripserit:

CVMQVE Mertonensem verissimum se praestiterit, moribus Mertonensibus per annos duos imbutus, usui et consuetudinibus iuvenum studiosorum Mertonensium laetissime obsecutus:

CVMQVE Universitas nostra Oxoniensis nec non Collegia eius cum Societatibus virisque doctis Nipponensibus vinculis amicitiae permultis iam coniuncta sint: NOS ERGO, doctrinam eius et diligentiam studiosam atque adeo summam erga Universitatem Oxoniensem pietatem monstratam admirati, in frequenti Congregationis Domo praedictum Principem Regalem DOCTOREM in Iure Civili renuntiamus eumque vi ac virtute huius Diplomatis omnibus iuribus et privilegiis adficimus quae ad hunc gradum spectant.

IN CVIVS REI TESTIMONIVM sigillum Universitatis quo hac in parte utimur adponendum curavimus.

Datum in Domo nostra Congregationis die XVIII° mensis Septembris A. S. MCMXCI.

HIS IMPERIAL HIGHNESS
CROWN PRINCE NARUHITO OF JAPAN

THE CHANCELLOR, MASTERS, AND SCHOLARS
OF THE UNIVERSITY OF OXFORD
TO WHOMSOEVER THESE PRESENTS
SHALL COME MAY THE LORD
EVER PRESERVE AND KEEP YOU

WHEREAS it has long been our custom to honour distinguished foreign Emperors, Kings, and Princes, especially those who have won fame by their fine character and by their learning:

AND WHEREAS His Imperial Highness NARUHITO, Crown Prince of Japan, has great experience of university life and work, and also of the Oxfordshire countryside, having served his academic apprenticeship in Japan and continued his studies at Oxford, where he wrote a substantial and scholarly account of the use of the Thames as a waterway for barges in the eighteenth century:

AND WHEREAS he is a true Mertonian, steeped in the traditions of Merton College for two years, when he happily shared in the undergraduate life of the College:

AND WHEREAS Oxford University and its Colleges are now linked by many friendly ties with Japanese companies and scholars:

NOW THEREFORE WE, admiring his learning and zest for academic work and his loyalty to the University of Oxford, do here in this full House of Congregation proclaim the aforesaid Crown Prince a DOCTOR in our Faculty of Civil Law, and by the force and virtue of this Diploma do hereby invest him with all privileges and rights of this Degree.

IN WITNESS WHEREOF we have caused to be affixed to this instrument the Seal of the University thereunto pertaining.

Given in our House of Congregation on the eighteenth day of September in the Year of Salvation 1991.

CAROLVS POPPER

ANNOS abhinc sexaginta studia hic de rebus physicis et philosophicis pariter alibi exercuit, id quod nunc demum licet iuventuti in Universitate Oxoniensi studiosae. sed minime coram hoc ausim praedicere gentem novam Popperianam nos necessario creaturos esse; adeo cuique propria et paene divina est res inveniendi facultas: ipse dixit quem honoramus.

Etenim multa de hac re docuit quae et amplissima sunt et permultis facile intelligibilia. negat autem rerum inventorem multis rebus observatis 'inductione', ut vocatur, uti. omnia enim non potest observare, cui quaedam eligenda sint quae observet. itaque in inventione rerum aliquid hic subesse docet quod rationi non sit consentaneum, nempe propriam cuiusque intellegentiam quae ipsa notiones creare valeat. in rerum naturae scientia *ingens* esse *decus, maximam amplitudinem* conscripsit. rationi autem cuivis et disciplinae meliorem rationem disciplinamque potiorem posse semper succedere, velut rationem hanc Einstinianam rationi illi Newtonianae. aptissime quidem laudavit versus illos Xenophanis:

οὔτοι ἀπ' ἀρχῆς πάντα θεοὶ θνητοῖς ὑπέδειξαν,
ἀλλὰ χρόνῳ ζητοῦντες ἐφευρίσκουσιν ἄμεινον.

Ut talia studia, talis inquisitio floreant opus est societate, quod aiunt, aperta; qua re fortis est hic pro libertate civili propugnator. omnium vero maxime interest quod falsum esse demonstravit mutationes illas quibus civitates adficiantur certis legibus esse praedicandas. Platoni autem quod auctoritatis severioris fautor esset obiecit, neque hoc displicet aequalibus nostris libros eius de Republica et de Legibus scriptos legentibus. exordio tamen hoc usus impetum in Carolum Marx, auctorem nostri saeculi praepotentem, fecit, doctrinam eius argumentis dilucidis refutavit. floret enim maxime in societate consaepta doctrina Marxiana, qua tot iam populi iacent oppressi tamquam 'gravi sub religione'. etenim philosophiae ipsius prius hac oppressae iamque liberae documentum vividum in Collegio tuo, Illustrissime, invenies. 'nolite divinationem falsam cauponari', dixit hic: 'fata ipsi vestra exercete.' nonne licet verba etiam illa de Epicuro quondam scripta de hoc viro usurpari?

religio pedibus subiecta vicissim
obteritur, nos exaequat victoria caelo.

Praesento vobis Carolum Popper, Equitem Auratum, Academiae Britannicae Societatisque Regiae pariter Socium, Professorem in Universitate Londiniensi emeritum, ut admittatur honoris causa ad gradum Doctoris in Litteris.

SIR KARL POPPER
Philosopher

SIXTY years ago in Vienna Sir Karl Popper studied Physics and Philosophy in parallel. Now at last it is possible for an Oxford student to do the same; but I would not dare to predict in the presence of our honorand that we will necessarily produce a crop of young Poppers: so individual and virtually God-given is the faculty of scientific discovery, as Popper himself has maintained.

There are many things in his teaching about scientific discovery which are both profound and generally intelligible. It is wrong to suppose that the scientist proceeds by induction from empirical observation, for he cannot observe everything: all observation is selective. Scientific discovery contains an irrational element, a certain 'creative intuition' or individual and unpredictable insight. Popper writes with a remarkable awareness of 'the greatness and the beauty of science', and he perceives that every scientific theory may be ultimately replaced by a better one, as Einstein's theory has largely replaced Newton's. He has aptly quoted the lines of Xenophanes:

> The gods did not reveal from the beginning
> All things to us, but in the course of time
> Through seeking we may learn and know things better.

Such free investigation and criticism can only flourish in an 'open society' and Popper strongly supports free institutions. Of importance to everybody is his refutation of the assumption that historical development is predictable and must follow certain laws of development. He has attacked the authoritarian and totalitarian attitude of Plato, which is evident to any modern reader of the *Republic* or *Laws*. But this is just the prelude to a rational refutation of the most influential of modern thinkers, Karl Marx, whose doctrines – that 'heavy dogma' by which so many peoples of the world are now oppressed – indeed flourish in a 'closed society'. In Balliol, your own College, Sir, you will find a lively instance of Philosophy herself recently freed from the oppression of this dogma.

'Instead of posing as prophets we must become the makers of our fate.' I quote from the end of *The Open Society and its Enemies*. We would be justified in using another quotation to describe the work of this honorand. Here are the words Lucretius once applied to Epicurus:

> The scruples of dogma which bound us he trampled underfoot.
> His victory exalts men to the skies.

I present Sir Karl Popper, FBA, FRS, Professor Emeritus in the University of London, for admission to the Honorary Degree of Doctor of Letters.

1982

NORMANNVS FOSTER RAMSEY

PHYSICUM hunc praeclarissimum invocatione Lucretiana *rerum inventorem* decet salutare; qui in Universitate magna Columbiana nec non apud Cantabrigienses nostros educatus, ad Cantabrigienses alteros reversus Professor in Universitate Harvardiana annos quadraginta duos fuit. per bellum Germanicum secundum ducibus Americanis insigne subvenit, quippe qui viros doctos vim atomorum adhibendam curantes adiuvaret. exinde physicis permultis primordia rerum varie indagantibus diu praefectus est. civitatum etiam foedere Atlantico coniunctarum consiliarius in annum electus est.

Praemio Nobeliano nuperrime nobilitatus est ob MASER atomicum inventum. ἐκχύσεις vero vel radios atomorum molecularumque hydrogenicarum ingeniosissime percontatus, atomos singulos subtilitate maxima inquisivit quo modo se gererent. horologium exinde omnibus quae umquam facta erant accuratius veriusque tempus metiendi causa fabricatus est, motibus quibusdam usus qui intra atomos hydrogenicos fiunt, **M**omentis adhibitis **A**mplificatis **S**timulata **E**missione virium **R**oentgenianarum.

Praeclarissime vero hoc inventum est. sunt tamen qui censent ponderis etiam plus habere experimenta quaedam de neutris elegantissime excogitata.

Particulam enim quam *neutron* vocamus virium electricarum expertem esse ab Orbilio pueros docente per annos iam quadraginta didicimus. idem ab Oratore nostro Iacobum Chadwick neutrorum inventorem laudante olim audivimus. experimenta tamen hic alia ingeniosissima instituit ad momentum duplex exiguum in neutro reperiendum excogitata. inde fortasse vires quasdam electricas neutro inesse tandem constabit, id quod physici qui res ratione tantum indagant suspicati sunt, nondum tamen invenerunt. o tempora! o mores! ἄνω ποταμῶν ἱερῶν χωροῦσι παγαί. manifestum iam fit quod scripsit olim Vergilius:

> pinguia corticibus sudent *electra* myricae.

nempe physicis nullis nisi τοῖς ἀκροτάτοις datur licentia scientiae suae labefactandae. nolite tamen doctrinam Orbili statim dediscere; nondum perfecta sunt haec experimenta: *adhuc sub iudice lis est.*

Apud nos bis diu peregrinatus (nam Professor Eastmannianus quondam fuit) Oxoniensibus bene notus est, quin etiam fabulosus. de quo cum memoriae tradita sint nonnulla, fabellam quandam bona vestra cum venia repetam.

Cum olim Oxonia Londinium iter faciebat, in vehiculo *omnibus* communi sedens, in sermonem alacriorem cum physico altero ingressus, a gubernatore subito interpellatus est: 'nisi desines rixari exeundum tibi erit.' tanto fervore, tanta vi de rebus physicis solet disputare.

Praesento vobis Normannum Ramsey, rerum inventorem, Scientiae Doctorem laboris causa iam creatum, Collegii Balliolensis quondam Socium, Praemio Nobeliano nomismatibus honoribus aliis permultis ornatum, ut admittatur honoris causa ad gradum Doctoris in Iure Civili.

NORMAN FOSTER RAMSEY
Physicist

IT is proper to welcome this outstanding physicist with a salute from Lucretius as *rerum inventor*, 'pioneer in Science'. He was educated at Columbia University and Cambridge (England), and eventually crossed over to Cambridge (Massachusetts) and was Higgins Professor at Harvard University for 42 years. During the war he served with distinction as a member of the group of scientists engaged in making use of atomic power. Thereafter he has for long presided over several groups of physicists, working on various properties of atoms. In 1958-9 he was Scientific Adviser to NATO.

Professor Ramsey has recently won a Nobel Prize for his invention of an atomic MASER. He conducted most ingenious experiments with rays of molecules and atoms and studied the working of single atoms of hydrogen with extreme precision. The MASER he designed is the most accurate timekeeper or clock ever known, based on motions within the hydrogen atom, using **M**icrowave **A**mplification by **S**timulated **E**mission of **R**adiation.

Though this was indeed a great discovery, there are some scholars who judge that certain elegant experiments of his on the neutron are of greater consequence.

For the past forty years we have been taught at school by Mr. Chips that the particle we call the 'neutron' carries no electric charge. In 1951 we were assured of this by our Orator when he presented Sir James Chadwick, who discovered the neutron. But now Professor Ramsey is involved in another set of highly ingenious experiments, designed to detect a minute dipole moment in the neutron. This would indicate the presence of electric charges, which theoreticians have suspected, but have not yet been able to detect. Really, the times are out of joint, 'the sacred rivers are running upstream'. At last we realise what Virgil meant when he wrote: 'Now we may find *electrons* dripping even from the tamarisk trees.' It is clear that only the topmost physicists are able to turn their science upside down. However, do not hurry to unlearn what Mr. Chips taught you at school. The experiments are still incomplete: the case is *sub judice*.

Professor Ramsey has made two substantial visits to Oxford (he was Eastman Professor in 1973–4) so that he is well-known to Oxford scholars, indeed legendary. From our stock of stories I will with your permission relate one.

He was once seated in a 'bus travelling from Oxford to London, engaged in a vigorous discussion with another physicist. Suddenly he was interrupted by the driver: 'If you don't stop quarrelling you'll have to get off my 'bus.' Such is the forcefulness and warmth which he brings to arguments about Physics.

I present Norman Ramsey, pioneer in Science, who has already won the conventional degree of Doctor of Science by submission of his work, formerly Fellow of Balliol College, whose achievement has been recognized by a Nobel Prize, by medals, and by many other honours, for the Honorary Degree of Doctor of Civil Law.

1990

SVIATOSLAVVS RICHTER

QUID, quaeso, inest praestantissimis illis fidicinibus qui nervos malleolis pulsant praeter ingenium per vim suam formidolosum a natura insitum cum diligentia maxima et laboriosa coniunctum? necesse est accedat vis quaedam divina ut ἔνθεοι esse videantur in modum vatis illius Homerici qui ὁρμηθεὶς θεοῦ ἄρχετο, φαῖνε δ᾽ ἀοιδήν. paucis tamen haec inest, quos eodem modo nosmet honestare debemus quo principes epici ἀοιδόν illum ἐρίηρον fovebant.

Latitabat diu vis huius divina in Foederatione Sovetica terrisque Europae ad orientem versis abscondita. rumores tantum interdum audiebamus de recitationibus mirabilibus, de mysteriis ibi perfectis, de ἐπόπταις, Russicis qui participes fuerant, θεοῦ πνοαῖσιν ἐμμανεῖς. fabulosa haec erant nec facile probanda. cum tamen abhinc triginta fere annos Londini recitationes habuit, eadem perturbatione, eadem animi concitatione turbam audientium commovit. *quid multa? clamores.* Cantabrigiae postea eodem modo postquam Ludovici maximi sonatam maximam in Collegio Regio repraesentaverat, non permiserunt audientes ut abiret. etenim cognovimus nosmet ipsi musicam hunc non repetere sed invenire ingenio tam subtili, tam intenso ut pars quaeque ex tempore excogitata esse videatur, ita tamen ut operis totius οἰκονομία clarissime omnibus appareat.

Subest nempe ei nervos pulsanti ferocia quaedam Russica, disciplina Germanica cohibita et formata. pater enim Theophilus, qui musicae elementa eum docuit, Vindobonae olim diu habitaverat; postea in Schola musica Moscuensi a magistro austero, Henrico Neuhaus, doctrina Germanorum severa imbutus est. sic tandem vim prodigiosam quae in manu sinistra inest comparavit comparatamque moderatus est.

Musicorum permultorum opera solet modulari, musicam in primis Schuberti, quam maxime diligit, Francisci Liszt, cuius sonatam unicam eximie interpretatus est, plurimorum denique qui classici vocantur. Sergio etiam Prokofiev opera componenti consilium dedit: sonatas eius sextam septimamque primus ad aures hominum protulit; nona huic est dicata. concentum eiusdem cum Mstislavo Rostropovich, quem decennium fere abhinc in hoc theatro honoravimus, tetrachordo primum modulante concinuit.

A Russicis suis saepe honestatus est, Ordini Leniniano adscriptus, praemio nomine eiusdem insigni nuper donatus, musicis omnibus Sovieticis a iudicibus summis quondam praelatus. musicus ipse, musicis natus, musicam duxit, quacum cantante saepe concinit.

Praesento vobis Sviatoslavum Richter, e populo musico virum μουσικώτατον, ut admittatur honoris causa ad gradum Doctoris in Musica.

SVIATOSLAV RICHTER
Musician

WHAT quality is there in pianists of the highest calibre apart from an astonishing natural genius, linked with 'an infinite capacity for taking pains'? They must also possess a mysterious divine force, so that they are seen to be God-inspired, like the Homeric bard who

> was aroused, began his God and showed forth song.

But this force is the possession of a very few, whom we must honour in the same way as epic heroes cherished that 'much-loved singer'.

For a long time Sviatoslav Richter's divine force lay hidden in the Soviet Union and the countries of Eastern Europe. In those days we had only occasional rumours about mysterious happenings at wonderful concerts, and about Russian initiates who attended, 'maddened by the breath of God'. Those stories were legendary and not easy to confirm. However, when at last some thirty years ago he gave concerts in London, the audiences were moved by the same emotion and mental disturbance. 'What follows needs no elaboration – cheers and shouts'. Later on after a performance of Beethoven's *Hammerklavier* Sonata at King's College, Cambridge, the audience just refused to let him leave. We in Britain have come to realise that our honorand does not reproduce a work of music: he creates it, and with a sheer ability which is so subtle and so intense that each section of a work appears to have been instantly invented, yet as part of a complete structure which is evident to everybody.

In his playing there is an underlying Russian wildness and savagery, restrained and shaped by German discipline. His father, Teofil Richter, who taught him the elements of music, had long lived in Vienna; later on in the Moscow Conservatory he was steeped in the austere training of the Germans by another strict teacher, Heinrich Neuhaus. Thus at last he developed and restrained the gigantic power of his left hand.

His repertoire is a wide one: Schubert, of whom he is particularly fond, Liszt, whose sonata he has brilliantly interpreted; and most of the classical composers. He advised Sergei Prokofiev when he was composing, and gave the first performance of his Sixth and Seventh Sonatas. The Ninth Sonata is dedicated to him. He accompanied Rostropovich, whom we honoured in this theatre ten years ago, when he played the 'cello in the first performance of Prokofiev's Symphony-Concerto.

He has received many Russian honours. He holds the Order of Lenin, and has recently won a Lenin Prize. He was placed first in the third Soviet Competition of Executant Musicians. As well as his father, his mother was a musician; so also is his wife, Nina, who often sings to his accompaniment.

I present Sviatoslav Richter, most eminent musician in a country of musicians, for the Honorary Degree of Doctor of Music.

1992

ANDREAS SAKHAROV

ANNOS abhinc centum decem Iohannem Turgenev in hoc theatro plausu maximo honoravimus, virum inter Russos suos populosque ceteros ob humanitatem notissimum, servorum Russicorum defensorem. Russum nunc alterum produco humanitate ubique illustrissimum, qui populum Sovieticum in libertatem vindicare nisus incommoda multa diu passus est. vindicem nempe summum videtis iurum illorum quae hominibus universis sunt communia.

Adest idem vir maxime peritus *rerum cognoscere causas*, Igoris Tamm discipulus, qui olim patriae defendendae causa belli instrumenta formidulosissima exquisivit: atomorum nempe leviorum nucleos, ut vocantur, calore fervidissimo commiscendos et conglutinandos curavit, ut per fusionem eorum vim ingentem proderet.

Sunt fortasse viri docti qui Prometheum hunc salutent, qui ignem Iovis secretum abstraxit. immo vero Minervae est similior, quae fulminibus Iovis potuit Furias conciliare, maluit tamen Πειθοῦς blanditias adhibere:

> κλῇδας οἶδα δώματος μόνη θεῶν
> ἐν ᾧ κεραυνός ἐστιν ἐσφραγισμένος.
> ἀλλ᾽ οὐδὲν αὐτοῦ δεῖ.

Pacis certe annos iam triginta propugnator salutari debet. etenim studia militaria diu aversus originem potius mundi totius indagavit, de concordia populorum paranda, de salute Sovieticorum istorum qui cum viris principibus dissentiebant multa pronuntiavit. audite, quaeso, exordium libelli primi ab Andrea Sakharov conscripti inter cives Sovieticos annos abhinc unum et viginti clam pervulgati:

> gentium discidium gentibus intentat exitium.

quae verba simplicia et dilucida memoria sunt dignissima, vox veritatis atque humanitatis qua nulla clarior inter multos annos e Russia evaserat. laetissime igitur a populis Europae occidentalis Americaeque accepta sunt. ecce praenuntius animi illius aperti qui nunc a Russis permultis laudatur.

Cuius animi signum esse credimus quod hospes hic noster in hoc theatro nunc adest, adest quoque uxor Helena, quae praelectionem eius Nobelianam apud Osloenses olim pronuntiavit: nam praemio Nobeliano ob pacem servatam honorato patria non licuit tunc ei egredi ut acciperet. o tempora nunc in melius mutata! o mores emendatos! adscitus nuper est concilio legatorum a populo isto electorum. sperare nunc demum licet cives multos quorum patronus hic et propugnator exstitit liberatum iri, inter populos foederatos Sovieticos populumque nostrum concordiam diuturnam futuram esse atque adeo amicitiam.

Praesento vobis Andream Sakharov, virum φυσικώτατον, Academiae Scientiarum Sovieticae diu adscriptum Praesidioque eiusdem iam adscitum, concordiae fautorem nobilissimum, ut admittatur honoris causa ad gradum Doctoris in Scientia.

ANDREI SAKHAROV
Physicist

THERE was great applause in this Theatre at the Encaenia of 1879 when we honoured Ivan Turgenev, who was famous in his native Russia and the rest of the world for his broad and liberal humanity and spoke up for the Russian serfs. Here now is another Russian whose humanity is celebrated everywhere, who has for long worked for freedom in the Soviet Union and indeed suffered much for his work. You see before you a supreme champion of human rights.

Andrei Sakharov is also a scientist who can 'discover the cause of things'. He was a pupil of Igor Tamm, and his early research involved the production of a terrifying weapon of war for the defence of his country. He succeeded in welding together the nuclei of some very light atoms by the application of intense heat, a fusion which produced immense energy.

Some scholars would salute Dr Sakharov as Prometheus, who stole the secret fire of Zeus. But I would rather compare him with Athena, who had it in her power to use Zeus' thunderbolts to win over the Furies, but preferred instead to use the blandishments of Persuasion:

> Alone of the gods I know that chamber's keys
> Where lies the thunder sealed and stored away.
> But there's no need of it.

Our honorand must be recognized as a champion of peace for the last thirty years. He long ago abandoned military research, and has instead worked on cosmology, investigating the origins of the universe. He has spoken frequently about harmony among nations and the welfare of political dissenters in Russia. Here is the beginning of his first Manifesto of 1968, which was secretly circulated in Russia. :

> The division of mankind threatens its destruction.

These lucid and simple words ought to be committed to memory. This was the clearest utterance of truth and humanity which had escaped from Russia for many years, and was accordingly received with joy by the peoples of Western Europe and America. Here was the harbinger of the *glasnost* which is now praised by so many Russians.

It is a sign of that *glasnost*, we believe, that Dr. Sakharov is now present in this theatre as our guest, together with his wife Yelena, who once delivered his Nobel lecture in Oslo, when after winning the Nobel Prize for Peace he was not allowed to leave his country to receive it. *O tempora! o mores!* Both the times and the attitudes have much improved. Recently he has been elected to the Congress of People's Deputies. Now at last we may hope that all those fellow-citizens whose cause he has promoted will be freed, and that there will be harmony and indeed friendship between our people and the peoples of the Soviet Union.

I present Andrei Sakharov, an outstanding physicist, who has long been an Academician of the Soviet Academy of Sciences and now is a member of its Praesidium, a noble champion of harmony, for the Honorary Degree of Doctor of Science.

1989

RICARDVS HENRICVS SALT

PROVIDENTIAE et munificentiae Gulielmi Morris, Baronis de Nuffield, multa debemus, hoc tamen in primis quod peritia medicaminum somnificorum et artium Lethaearum maxime praestamus Oxonienses, quarum scientiam per orbem terrarum diffundimus. famam enim magnam et Universitati et urbi huic contulit *evaporator* iste *Oxoniensis,* a medicis physicisque nostris inventus, quo vapores diversos certe et accurate metiri licuit; quorum tria fere milia in officinis suburbanis prope Bovillas nostras sitis ab eodem Gulielmo Morris fabricata sunt, qui quingentos legionibus dono dedit.

Rei huius optime gestae pars magna fuit vir quem nunc produco. per annos enim triginta novem quidquid medici illi Lethes moderatores excogitaverant artificio suo fingebat. chirurgos etiam in valetudinario eodem laborantes adiuvabat, quippe qui promptus esset ad praestandum

> quidquid in arte sua potuit promittere curae,
> quod fieri ferro liquidove potest electro.

id quod Professori novo Nuffieldensi maxime proderat. neque cum demum artificibus compluribus praefectus rude donatus est libellos conscribere desivit; etenim operam tunc ad Museum apparatuum comparandum dedit, quod in valetudinario altero Iohannis Radcliffe licet intueri.

Ecce *evaporatores* et pristini et recentiores, et multiplices et simplices, quorum unus recentissime spectatus est in certamine Martio, a medicis legionariis doctrina huius institutis adhibitus. *laminas* deinde inspicite faucibus nostris ab hoc accommodatas et luminibus minutissimis instructas, quibus vocis ipsa origo intuenti pateat, quae Abendoniae fabricatae latissime per mundum dimittuntur. fornaculam vero in officina sua instituit, qua *fistulas* has e laticibus Indis formatas calefecit duravitque ut molestiam flexu subito quam minime obferrent; maximi quidem momenti hoc est eis quibus hae tamquam spiramenta in fauces insertae sunt. accedunt *acus* subtiliores, corporis pungendi causa factae, quorum in latere foramina insunt quae liquoribus introitum modo permittunt, dum exitum prohibent.

Multa quoque contulit hic ad societatem instituendam eorum qui artium eiusmodi periti sunt, **S**ocietatem scilicet **A**rtificum **L**ethes, quo in titulo SAL quoddam invenire possitis. praelectio etiam quae apud sodales huius societatis interdum habetur nomine eius est insignis.

Praesento vobis Ricardum Henricum Salt, artificibus quondam praefectum, ut admittatur honoris causa ad gradum Magistri in Artibus.

RICHARD HENRY SALT
Scientific technician

NOT the least of the many debts we owe to William Morris, Lord Nuffield, is the pre-eminence of Oxford in the study of anaesthetics, a science which we propagate throughout the world. Both the University and the City of Oxford have won great fame from the *Oxford Vaporizer,* invented by our doctors and physicists. This allowed a controlled concentration of gases in anaesthesia. Nearly three thousand of these were made by Morris himself in his factory at the Oxford suburb of Cowley, and he gave five hundred to the Forces.

Our honorand Mr Richard Salt played a great part in the achievement of this success. For thirty-nine years his technical skill gave shape to the work of the Nuffield Department of Anaesthetics. Moreover, the surgeons at the Radcliffe found him a most helpful neighbour, ready to provide

> All that his art and care could promise them,
> Whatever steel and molten ore can make.

This greatly smoothed the path of the new Nuffield Professor. When Mr Salt eventually retired as Senior Chief Technician he did not stop publishing articles in the journals. Indeed he devoted his energies to the creation of a Museum of Anaesthetic Apparatus which may be inspected in the John Radcliffe Hospital.

Here are *vaporizers,* ancient and modern, complex and simplified, one of which was recently battle-tested in the Falklands war by anaesthetists who had been briefed by Richard Salt. Next examine these laryngoscope *blades,* precisely shaped by our honorand to fit the human throat, and fitted with tiny bulbs to allow inspection of the vocal chords. They are manufactured in Abingdon and despatched all over the world. Mr Salt installed an oven in his workshop to bake those rubber endotracheal *tubes* to the right toughness to render them 'non-kinking' – a matter of consequence for the patients who have them inserted into their windpipes. Then there are delicate *needles* for injection, with lateral holes fitted with one-way valves.

Mr Salt has also played a big part in setting up a professional association of technicians with similar interests, the **S**ociety of **A**naesthetic **L**aboratory **T**echnicians with the ingenious acronym SALT. The Fellows of the Society have established a regular Salt Lecture, named after him.

I present Richard Henry Salt, formerly Senior Chief Technician, for admission to the Honorary Degree of Master of Arts.

1984

CAECILIA SAUNDERS

LUMINA PLURA PARA! Iohannis Wolfgang de Goethe morientis haec, ut traditur, verba novissima fuerunt. neque aliter heros ille Homericus deum precatus est: ἐν δὲ φάει καὶ ὄλεσσον. eis enim qui morbo diuturno adfecti moribundi iacent maximi momenti est ab adiutrice foveri qualis haec est, quae plurimis et aegerrimis tamquam lux in tenebris esse videatur.

Licet enim, licet mortem decenter obire salva dignitate quae homines decet, si modo doctrinam ab hac inventam animadvertimus. cura tali sustineri magnopere optandum est non solum Christianis, quibus mors ianua vitae erit, sed eis etiam quibus spes tantum est talia futura esse. ita adlevandi sunt aegroti ut vita quae supersit secure fruantur, cum medicamentis satis sollerterque adhibitis, tum tranquillitate nescioqua laetitiaque quam ministrae fide Christiana sustentatae prae se ferunt.

Consilium quondam haec cepit ut valetudinarium vel refugium aedificaret eis idoneum qui morbo mortifero adflicti essent. hoc ut adsequeretur qualia excogitare machinari perficere debuit, quantam pecuniam congerere, quot homines in unum cogere monere sollicitare! quae omnia dum aegris alibi simul adsidet agenda erant. dubitanti sententia e libris sacris quasi sors oblata est:

> Revela Domino viam tuam et spera in Eo et Ipse faciet.

qua corroborata omnia peregit. refugio Sancto Christophoro consecrato nomen bene ominatum *hospitii* datum est.

Pedetemptim ad haec facienda progressa est, quae studiis primis Oxoniensibus propter bellum dilatis artis medicinae iam adulta Londini studia fecit eo consilio ut moribundos foveret.

Nonnulla autem de moribundos adlevandi arte scripsit, quam indagando augendam aliisque tradendam in hospitio suo curavit. hospitia iam exstant complura, quorum fundatores ipsa consilio iudicioque solet adiuvare; etenim hospitio Oxoniensi discipulus huius praefectus est. nonne et vigilantiae pro aegris eximiae causa et illuminationis quam disseminavit cum Florentia nostra lucifera comparanda est?

Praesento vobis Caeciliam Saunders, Excellentissimi Ordinis Imperii Britannici Dominam Commendatricem, Collegii Regii Medicinae Sodalem, Collegii nostri Sanctae Annae honoris causa Sociam, ut admittatur honoris causa ad gradum Doctoris in Iure Civili.

DAME CICELY SAUNDERS
Hospice founder

MEHR LICHT! By tradition these were the last words of Goethe, comparable with the prayer of the Homeric hero: 'Kill us if you will, but kill us in the light.' It is of the first importance that those who lie dying of slow terminal diseases should be cared for by a nurse or physician like Dame Cicely Saunders, who has been able to lighten the darkness of many sick people.

It is indeed possible for such a patient to meet death in a fitting manner, without losing his proper human dignity. This can be achieved if only we pay attention to the discipline which our honorand has instituted. Such care is deeply and properly desired, not only by Christians who regard death as the gateway to Life, but also by those who merely hope that something akin to the Christian's expectation will happen after death. The sick must be effectively relieved so that they can enjoy without anxiety what life is left to them. This relief is produced by a skilful and adequate dosage of drugs, backed up by that indefinable atmosphere of calm and joy which shines forth from medical attendants who are sustained by a lively Christian faith.

Cicely Saunders made a decision to build a hospital or place of refuge for patients with terminal diseases. Imagine the plans that had to be devised and carried through, the funds that had to be raised, the people who had to be brought together, briefed, and pressed to help. All this had to be done while she was still looking after sick people elsewhere. In a moment of doubt she consulted the text for the day and found this for her guidance:

> Commit thy way unto the Lord; trust also in
> Him and He shall bring it to pass.

This text gave her strength, and she persevered and achieved her plan. Her hospital was dedicated to St Christopher and given a name of good omen, *hospice,* or place of refreshment.

Her progress to this achievement was slow: she advanced gradually step by step. Her first studies in Oxford, at the Society for Home Students, were interrupted by the war, and it was in London as a mature student that she took her medical qualification with the definite intention of working for dying patients.

Cicely Saunders has published several books and articles on the care of the dying, and has taken care to make provision in St Christopher's Hospice for research and teaching in this field. There are now a number of such hospices, whose founders she has advised and assisted; one of her pupils is now Director of Michael Sobell House in Oxford. Must we not compare her with another woman, Florence Nightingale, who shed much light and expended vast energy in organising the care of the sick?

I present Dame Cicely Saunders, DBE, FRCP, Honorary Fellow of St Anne's College, for the Honorary Degree of Doctor of Civil Law.

1986

GEORGIVS SOROS

AQUINCI hic natus, Londini a Carolo Popper nonnulla de civitate illa aperta doctus, strenue per multos annos desudavit ut populi Hungariae suae atque adeo Europae totius orientalis dominatione ista nostri saeculi saevissima et eadem maxime diuturna apud Russos primum orta, a Russis inde aggravata, liberarentur. cuius libertatis imminentis erat praenuntius. fundationem enim quondam transatlanticam instituit nomine civitatis apertae insignem; alias deinde in Hungaria Polonia Foederatione Sovietica, quae discipulos adiuvarent ad studia nova atque insueta domi facienda, libros in bibliothecis peregrinis legendos, cum academicis alienigenis disputandum. itaque studiosis plurimis momentum hic est et causa migrationis. nam scholares Hungaros Polonos Russos a nomine suo appellatos Oxoniam per annos iam quattuor mittit: quinquaginta nunc in Collegiis nostris studia exercentes invenietis, adiuvantibus et Collegiis et Reginae nostrae Ministris; qui et disciplinis nostris et civitatibus suis magnopere iam profuerunt. nonne aptissime eum comparabitis cum alumno nostro Gulielmo Fulbright, decore illo Senatus Americani, qui copiam nobis Americanorum ingeniosorum diu praebet?

Fundationes tantas quo modo, rogabitis, opibus suppeditat? nempe annos viginti unum pecunias et suas et alienas Novi Eboraci augendas curavit, mutationes collybi pretiorumque accuratissime observando. certiores de hoc facti mirabimini *quantum* sit ei providentiae, *quantum* de re pecuniaria sollertiae, *quantum* porro incrementum pecuniis illis accederit.

Qua experientia fretus ratione tota vendendi emendique philosophorum in modum indagata librum conscripsit cui titulum *De arte magica argentariorum* χρύσεα χαλκείων *permutantium* ideo dedit quod peritiam hanc scientiam veram esse negat: nimia enim ex improviso fieri, ex illo ipso quod rationem aliquis indaget rationem ipsam mutari, *reversione,* ut vocat, facta. ἴτην hunc esse censemus, qui celerrime excogitat, excogitata celerrime exsequitur.

> πάρεστι δ' ἔργον ὡς ἔπος
> σπεῦσαι τι τῶν βούλιος φέρει φρήν.

quid? fundationes nuperrime in Boiohaemia, apud populos Codanos, apud Scythas denique aliasque gentes Ponticas aut instituit aut corroboravit. libertatis insuper fautoribus qui civitatibus his praefecti sunt consilium de rebus oeconomicis iam dedit. opportunissime vero nobis oblatus est Europam novam liberamque fingentibus.

Praesento vobis Georgium Soros, Scholae Oeconomicorum Londiniensis alumnum, Europaeorum plurimorum benefactorem, ut admittatur honoris causa ad gradum Doctoris in Iure Civili.

GEORGE SOROS
Financier and Philanthropist

GEORGE SOROS was born in Budapest and learned about the Open Society from Professor Karl Popper in the London School of Economics. He worked hard for many years to help to free his fellow Hungarians and also the whole of eastern Europe from what was once the most savage and prolonged tyranny of our age, which, having started in Russia, was made more burdensome by the Russians: he was a harbinger of their present freedom. He began long ago by setting up an 'Open Society Foundation' in the United States. There followed other Foundations in Hungary, Poland, and the Soviet Union, intended to assist students to undertake independent projects in their own countries and to enable them to read in foreign libraries and to hold discussions with foreign scholars.

In this way it has come about that Mr Soros is a motivating force which has caused many students to travel and work abroad. For four years now he has been sending Soros Scholars from Hungary, Poland, and the Soviet Union to Oxford. There are now fifty to be found pursuing their studies in Oxford colleges, with the cooperation of the colleges and of HM Government. The Soros scholars have already done much to benefit their Oxford departments and their own countries. It is appropriate to compare George Soros with an Oxford man, Senator James William Fulbright, who has for long been providing Oxford with an abundant and able crop of Fulbright Scholars.

You may well ask how he funds these large Foundations. The answer is that for twenty-one years he has been managing a mutual fund in New York, increasing his own investments and those of his investors by careful attention to the changes in the stock market and the exchange rates. When you learn of the history of the Quantum Fund you will wonder at his foresight, his financial skill, and the sheer increase in the value of this Fund.

He has used the experience he has gained from the Quantum Fund to investigate the whole business of buying and selling from a philosophical point of view. The result is a book *The Alchemy of Finance*, thus ironically entitled because he does not believe that he is writing about a true science: there are too many unexpected occurrences, and by the principle of 'reflexivity' the presence of an investigator at any process alters the process itself.

We welcome him as a man with 'go' in him, who thinks fast and acts fast.

> Quick as his word comes action, urging on
> Whatever plans his active mind devises.

What next? Very recently he has extended his Foundation activities to Czechoslovakia, the Baltic States, and the Black Sea nations – Bulgaria, Romania, and the Ukraine. He has, moreover, been consulted by several governments in central Europe which desire greater economic freedom. Now that we are creating a new, free Europe his presence and his help are most timely.

I present George Soros, a graduate of the London School of Economics, a benefactor of many citizens of Europe, for the Honorary Degree of Doctor of Civil Law.

1990

IOANNA SUTHERLAND

SAEPENUMERO in cantatrice praesentanda veritus sum ne gratius et iucundius sit vobis illam ipsam audire carmen canentem qualem Graecorum heroes olim audiebant,

κηληθμῷ δ'ἔσχοντο κατὰ μέγαρα σκιόεντα.

sed legibus Congregationis inveteratis consaepti sumus et impediti:

nulli fas nunc cantare.

Cantatricem nunc produco e partibus Australibus praeclarissimam, sive Ioannam decet vocare sive Luciam, ut memoriae plurimorum tradita est. aliis vero Domina Anna est, aliis Lucretia, aliis Semele vel Domina Elvira. maxime tamen audientes commovit cantu illo quem ultimum apud Hortos nostros Londinienses cantavit, ut populo audienti valediceret. fabula enim melica tunc agebatur Iohannis Strauss quae *Vespertilio* inscripta est. ibi in coetu potatorum gaudentium ei placuit aliquid in Hortis illis inusitatum atque sibi proprium cantare, carmen illud aetatis prioris notissimum et blandissimum, de domum revertendi dulcedine. 'sibi proprium' dixi; sed rerum musicarum doctissimis hoc carmen in memoriam reduxit vocem Melbae (nam gratissimum ei fuerat), cantatricis illustrissimae omnium ante ipsam civium suarum, quae eodem anno audientibus valedixit quo haec est nata.

Nempe vox eius est purissima; quam ut exponam verba Vergiliana adhibebo:

igneus est illi vigor et caelestis origo.

itaque maxime est idonea fabulis illis melicis quas critici *bellissime cantabiles* vocant. etenim in fabulis gravioribus Donizetti Bellini Rossini frequentissime cantavit, quae hac cantante vigore quodam accepto renatae sunt.

Annus iam est quadragesimus ex quo primum in Hortis Londiniensibus cantavit. orbem iam terrarum cantu totum peragravit, apud Australenses suos bis cum coetu suo cantorum cecinit, nec non in Odeo illo recens aedificato quod inter miracula illa septem nunc decet numerari. cognomen autem ἡ θαυμασία a permultis ei est impositum, quamvis modestiam comitatem benevolentiam prae se ferat.

Praesento vobis Ioannam Sutherland, Ordini insigniter Meritorum adscriptam, Australiae Comitem, Excellentissimi Ordinis Imperii Britannici Dominam Commendatricem, ut admittatur honoris causa ad gradum Doctoris in Musica.

DAME JOAN SUTHERLAND
Singer

I have often, when presenting a singer, feared that you would prefer to hear the honorand herself singing a song such as the assembled Greek heroes once heard,

> held spellbound in their shadowy halls.

But we are prevented from this by the venerable rules of Congregation:

> Singing is now forbidden.

Our present honorand is an illustrious singer from Australia. I hesitate whether to call her Joan or Lucia, as many here may remember her. To some she is Donna Anna, to others Lucretia, or Semele, or Donna Elvira. But the performance which her audience found most touching was perhaps her farewell song at Covent Garden. The opera was *Die Fledermaus*. In the party scene she chose to sing a song appropriate to herself, one not usually heard at the Royal Opera House – that famous popular song of the Victorian age, *Home, Sweet Home*. I call this 'appropriate to herself', but to those of her audience who were knowledgeable about music it recalled the voice of the most renowned of all previous singers from Australia. It was the favourite song of Melba, who gave her farewell performance in the year of Joan Sutherland's birth.

Her voice is superlatively pure, and has what Virgil called

> The might of fire, sent from Heaven.

It is especially suited to operas of the *bel canto* category. She has indeed sung frequently in the serious operas of Donizetti, Bellini and Rossini, which have been reinvigorated by her singing and taken on new life.

It is forty years since she first sang at Covent Garden. Since then she has girdled the earth with song, revisiting Australia twice with a specially chosen group of singers, and performing notably in one of the seven modern Wonders of the World, the new Sydney Opera House. Many people know her as *La Stupenda,* a name which belies the fact that her modesty, courtesy, and kindness are manifest to all.

I present Dame Joan Sutherland, OM, AC, DBE, for the Honorary Degree of Doctor of Music.

1992

GEORGIVS THOMAS

FAVETE LINGUIS: solemnem et propriam huius precationem adhibeo, qua permultis iam est notus. qui si quando ad nos Oxonienses advenit sanguinis perturbatione quadam adficitur; dixit ipse cum sacra hic nuper praedicavit. maiore nunc trepidatione commotus sum qui hunc tibi, Illustrissime, praesento qui dignitatem prae se fert maximam senatus nostri venerabilis. eosdem tamen veneramur, Iohannem ego Pym, virum Pembrochiensem, fortissimum auctoritatis istius propugnatorem, Willelmum hic Lenthall, Oxoniensem alterum, qui illum coram rege verbis notissimis defendit. hic autem quem produco re vera est 'vir bonus dicendi peritus'; cui quamvis rerum publicarum experientia versato fides inest, 'vitro', ut aiunt, 'perlucidior'. doctrinam enim Domini Nostri praedicandam esse credit, praedicat ipse verbis simplicibus quibus inest vis Celtica quae tot homines in regionibus Hesperiis ortos oratores reddidit, expertis dico.

Natus enim in valle Rhondda, inter homines labore durissimo sudantes educatus, sub vexillo sanguinolento noluit militare, partes praetulit operariorum argumentis in senatu res agentium. etenim magna perfecit, rebus quondam consortionis nostrae nationum, deinde rebus Cambrensibus praefectus, Praeses tandem senatus pari omnium acclamatione electus.

Grammaticus autem fuerat, benignus nempe interdumque severus, qui pueros nominatim adhortabatur: 'euge papae', 'optime', eodem modo quo senatores qui tum primum sententiam dixerunt adhortatus est. apte quidem illud insigni suo adscriptum habet:

> Dux eris si conduxeris.

artes illo tempore ipse perdidicit quae maxime postea ad iras eleganter conponendas profuerunt. severitatem tunc iustissime adhibuit cum post controversiam turbulentiorem senatores auctoritate sua, ut licet, dimisit. coeunt rursus in curiam frequentes, temperati iam silent. brevissime tum Praeses, 'Tumultuose', dixit, 'res hodie acta est.' quo dicto senatores iterum de improviso dimisit. ecce Praesidis maximi auctoritas.

Praesento vobis virum praehonorabilem Georgium Thomas, Reginae ex Intimo Consilio, Senatus Prolocutorem emeritum, optimae matris filium optimum, ut admittatur honoris causa ad gradum Doctoris in Iure Civili.

GEORGE THOMAS

Speaker of the House of Commons

ORDER, ORDER. I make no apology for borrowing Mr Speaker's signature tune, familiar now to millions of people. Whenever George Thomas comes to Oxford he feels a tingling sensation; so he revealed in his recent University sermon. My own trepidation is greater, for I am presenting to you, Sir, an honorand who embodies for us the immense authority and power of our ancient House of Commons. We share the same heroes, however: I have great respect for John Pym, a Pembroke man who fought hard for the authority of Parliament; he honours Speaker Lenthall, also from Oxford, who defended Pym in the presence of King Charles I in words which have become famous. Moreover, this honorand is indeed 'a good man, skilled in speaking'. Despite all his political experience he has a faith which is 'more translucent than glass'. He believes that Our Lord's teaching must be preached, and preaches it himself in simple words spoken with the Celtic intensity which has produced so many orators from the West; you know what we're like.

George Thomas was born in the Rhondda valley and brought up among men who endured harsh toil and sweat. He rejected the Red Flag of communism, and chose instead the Parliamentary methods of the Labour Party. His achievements have indeed been great: he served as Minister of State in the Commonwealth Office, then as Secretary of State for Wales, and was eventually elected Speaker by the unanimous agreement of the main parties in the House.

In his early years as a schoolmaster 'he was kind' to be sure and yet 'severe' at times, addressing the boys in the same terms which he has been heard using to an MP making his maiden speech: 'Well done, Tommy, good man.' The inscription on his arms is certainly appropriate:

> Bid ben bid hont.

In school he acquired a skill which has been invaluable in deftly checking outbursts of anger. He brought his severity to bear very properly after an especially turbulent debate, when he adjourned the House by the exercise of his own powers. The Members flocked back, and sat subdued and silent. Speaker Thomas spoke briefly. 'There have been scenes of grave disorder here tonight,' he said, and adjourned the House unexpectedly a second time. Such is the authority of a great Speaker.

I present the Rt. Hon. George Thomas, PC, retiring Speaker of the House of Commons, a son worthy of his mother, for admission to the Honorary Degree of Doctor of Civil Law.

1983

EVA TURNER

IN *aula hac regali* – quae verba quanta auctoritate ab hac cantata licet audire – Dominam hanc multosque alios artibus musicis insignissimos audivimus, et quosdam ex eis honestavimus. quorum vix ullus honoribus est dignior hac quam nunc produco. inest enim rebus quas feliciter gessit vetustas prope fabulosa, quae Cancellario nostro maxime placebit. nam tempore prioris illius belli medio iuveni ei licuit hanc in fabella melica cantantem audire, vocem spei et salutis in anno Cannensi praenuntiam. meminimus nos iuniores vocem eius carmen sollemne de rege Georgio sexto eodem die inaugurato Londini canentis. postea in Hesperia nostra Hesperidum modo vocalium partes Aïdae in amphitheatro frequentissimo Pasadenae cecinit.

At quid opus est sermone meo pedestri? praescios versus repetam Catulli:

> saepe illam perhibent ardenti corde furentem
> clarisonas imo fudisse e pectore voces.

quae ne in altissima parte quidem cantus istius quem de aenigmatibus Turandotis cantavit claritate deficiebatur; durae silicis vires apte comparabant viri docti qui audiverant.

Partes autem illas in fabellis agebat in quibus summa vocis mobilitate et amplitudine opus erat, summa quoque histrionis arte, Aïdae, Turandotis, Bruenhildae. cuius de ingenio certiore facto ipso Toscaninio Mediolanum haec ad Scalam istam praestantissimam arcessita est. quid eo tempore inusitatius quam in fabellis Italicis apud ltalos Anglicam cantare? γλαῦκ' εἰς Ἀθήνας non inepte dicebant. at princeps erat Anglicarum nonnullarum quae magnam famam apud gentes externas adsecutae sunt. Turandotis autem partes per annos viginti egit apud populos diversissimos, Londini, Bononiae, in Venezuela, apud Chicagoenses. nempe Alfanius, qui post mortem Puccini opus illud perfecit, veram et absolutam imaginem Turandotis censuit eam praebere, qualem auctor ipse in animo habuisset.

Rude haec nunquam donata est, quae ad nova facienda mavult cursum vertere. officio enim fabellas agendi iam perfuncta docere coepit, in Universitate Oklahomae Professor vocis excolendae creata. ubi in spatium unius anni electa usque ad annum decimum primum mansit; via, ut dicitur, usa est. officium deinde simile Londini in Academia Regali Musicae, cuius est alumna, suscepit. docet nimirum etiam nunc, et Praeses est societatis ad honorem Ricardi Wagner institutae.

Praesento vobis Evam Turner, Excellentissimi Ordinis Imperii Britannici Dominam Commendatricem, Collegii Sanctae Hildae honoris causa Sociam, ut admittatur honoris causa ad gradum Doctoris in Musica.

DAME EVA TURNER
Singer

IN *questa reggia* – an opening which you may hear this honorand singing with immense authority – in this regal hall we have heard Eva Turner and many other distinguished musicians perform and we have conferred degrees on some of them. None is more worthy of this honour than Dame Eva. The triumphs of her career have an aura of history which comes close to the legendary and which our Chancellor will appreciate. As a young officer he could have heard her singing in opera in the middle of the first world war, a harbinger of hope and safety in the year of the Somme battles. My generation remembers her singing *God Save the King* at Covent Garden on the night of the coronation of King George VI. And in the far West she took on the role of the singing Hesperides and sang Aïda in 1938 to a packed stadium at Pasadena, California.

But the time has come to abandon prose for the prescient lines of Catullus:

> Often (they say) maddened by pangs of love
> A ringing voice she poured straight from her heart.

Even in the high phrases of the Riddle scene in *Turandot* she showed perfect clarity; the critics aptly wrote of a 'rock-like' quality in her voice.

She kept on singing parts which demanded both great flexibility and range of voice and acting ability: Aïda, Turandot, Brünhilde. Toscanini himself heard of her talent and she was summoned to Milan to sing at La Scala. At that time it was most unusual for an English woman to sing Italian opera in Italy; it was natural that people talked of sending *vasi a Samo,* coals to Newcastle. She became in fact the first of a number of English women singers to win a reputation overseas. She sang Turandot for twenty years in far-flung places, London, Bologna, Venezuela, Chicago. Alfano, who completed the opera after Puccini's death, considered her the ideal Turandot, such as the author had envisaged.

She has never retired: she prefers simply to change her mode of activity. When she stopped singing opera she began her career of teaching, as Visiting Professor of Voice Production at the University of Oklahoma. Having gone for one year she stayed for eleven; everything evidently went her way out there. Then she held a similar post at the Royal Academy of Music in London, of which she is an alumna. She is still, of course, teaching, and is President of the Wagner Society.

I present Eva Turner, DBE, Honorary Fellow of St Hilda's College, for admission to the Honorary Degree of Doctor of Music.

1984

MARGARETA TURNER-WARWICK

INEXORABILES esse dicuntur medici, qui non facile e consuetudinibus veteribus discedant. ἀλλ' ἐκδιδάσκει πάνθ' ὁ γηράσκων χρόνος. anno nuper centesimo vicesimo quarto ex quo Elizabethae Garrett Anderson a Collegio Regio Medicorum repulsae licuit tamen aegris mederi femina tandem Praeses eiusdem Collegii est creata; Margareta scilicet Turner-Warwick, quam nunc produco.

Ecce medica praeclarissima, quae aegris ipsis semper est benignissima. cuius rei causa non longe est quaerenda. nam discipula olim Oxoniensis pulmonum pthisi correpta per annum totum in lecto languit, itaque Vergilianum illud aptissime poterat repetere:

> non ignara mali miseris succurrere disco.

In nosocomio insignissimo Londiniensi Professor per annos quindecim fuit eius partis Medicinae quae thoraces curat: Decana eadem fuit, medicos docendi officio praefecta. plurima autem contulit ad sanandum vel cohibendum morbum istum quem *spiritus angustias* vel *anhelitum* vocant; quem gravissimum esse docuit, cuius causa diligentissime inquirenda esset, ut radicitus exstirparetur.

Praeses nunc creata Collegii Regii Medicorum, tirones in primis curat ut optime doceantur atque instituantur, instituti ut officiis medicorum quam optime fungantur. in rebus autem agendis comitate sua maxima solet uti, ita tamen ut tenax semper sit propositi. laboris nempe est amantissima, in modum ducis illius antiqui qui suis semper instabat,

> nil actum credens cum quid superesset agendum.

neque mirum hoc est; nam avunculus ei erat Robertus ille Baden-Powell, vir aetatis suae promptissimus, qui parsimonia temporis maxime abundabat. iuvenibus tamen tirocinium in medicina facientibus pro parte sua feminea nuper subvenit postulantibus ne laboribus continuis diutius exerceantur. officia etiam nuper suscepit Concilii novi fundati quod de rebus ethicis quae ad medicos pertinent institutum est.

Tirocinium ipsa apud nos egit, Aulae Dominae Margaretae adscripta, cuius nunc est Socia honoris causa. vult autem iam defuncta officiis otiose cum coniuge filiabus nepotibus versari. at non tunc expers erit rerum medicarum, ut quae et uxor sit et mater medicorum. speramus nosmet certe eam studium suum musicae exercentem concentus laetos cum nepotibus diutissime facturam esse.

Praesento vobis Margaretam Turner-Warwick, Excellentissimi Ordinis Imperii Britannici Dominam Commendatricem, Medicinae Doctorem, Aulae Dominae Margaretae Sociam honoris causa creatam, ut admittatur honoris causa ad gradum Doctoris in Scientia.

DAME MARGARET TURNER-WARWICK
Physician

DOCTORS, they say, are a conservative lot, who will not budge an inch from their traditional way of life.

But ageing Time teaches one everything.

Recently, in the 124th year after Elizabeth Garrett Anderson, rejected by the Royal College of Physicians, was licensed as a doctor to heal the sick, a woman was at last elected President of the Royal College, namely Margaret Turner-Warwick, our present honorand.

Here is an eminent doctor who is exceptionally and invariably kindly to her patients. The cause of this is not far to seek. As an Oxford undergraduate she contracted tuberculosis of the lungs and spent a whole year confined to bed; in the words of Dido,

From my own pain I learn to help the sick.

She was Professor of Thoracic Medicine for fifteen years at the Brompton Hospital, where she has also been Dean, in charge of the training of students. She has made an immense contribution to the management and care of asthma. She has emphasized that asthma is a most serious disease; and has insisted that great efforts must be made to discover its cause in order to eliminate it by medical treatment.

In her present post as President of the Royal College of Physicians she is especially concerned with the proper teaching and training of medical graduates and with the conduct of doctors. In all her dealings she makes great use of her charm, which is considerable, but without ever losing her grip on her objective. She is a glutton for work,

Thinking naught done while aught remained to do.

This is not strange, for she is a grand-niece of Robert Baden-Powell, the most energetic man of his age, who was particularly economical of his time. None the less, she recently supported the junior doctors in their campaign against excessively long spells of duty, and gave them all the help that was humanly possible. She has also recently undertaken to serve on a new Council for Bio-ethics in medicine.

She herself started her training in Oxford as an undergraduate at Lady Margaret Hall, of which she is now an Honorary Fellow. She now wishes on her retirement to spend more time with her husband, her children, and her grandchildren; but even then she will not be far from medical matters, for she is both the wife and the mother of doctors. We hope that she will long enjoy her musical pursuits and the chamber music she performs with her grandchildren.

I present Dame Margaret Turner-Warwick, DBE, DM, Honorary Fellow of Lady Margaret Hall, for the Honorary Degree of Doctor of Science.

1992

REVERENDISSIMVS DESMONDVS TUTU

ADEST tandem, adest vir cuius imaginem saepe domi vidimus, vocem procul proloquentis audivimus. ecce Fidei nostrae defensor, propugnator idem libertatis qui populorum totius Africae meridionalis universorum iura strenue tutatus est. hunc vero cum honoramus aliis simul honorem debemus conferre: *exercitum* illum *candidatum martyrum* decet laudare qui ubique iustitiae aequitatis pacis constituendae causa labores ingentes pertulerunt.

Aptissime hic comparatus est cum prophetis Iudaeorum antiquis, utpote qui quaecumque sunt vera, molesta licet viris primariis esse videantur, aperte soleat pronuntiare. cuius edictis maxime opus est. notissimum enim omnibus est *discidium* istud a principibus prioribus confectum inter Afros indigenas atque eos qui originem a gentibus Europaeis ducunt. discidium hoc nefandum (piget enim verbum ipsum infaustum atque abominandum enuntiare in theatro hoc artibus scientiisque humanioribus dicato) per vitam paene totam oppugnavit. quod cum attenuatum iam sit, non tamen exstinctum, id noster maxime quaerit ut sine bello debellet.

Londini autem quamvis in Collegio Regio theologiam doctus, in Anglia diu versatus, colore tamen quodam Africano mentem suam fucatam esse praedicat. imbutus enim est humanitate illa, amore illo disserendi, animi illa simplicitate quae gentibus Africanis propria esse censet. abest omnino severitas, abest ostentatio; huius certe *mentem mortalia tangunt.* quid? liberato nuper Mandela (quam liberationem maximi momenti esse omnes intelleximus) nonne Archiepiscopum ipsum vidimus *pede libero* tellurem pulsantem? laudanda tunc erant verba haud inepta Horatiana:

recepto / dulce mihi furere est amico.

plus valebat illa saltatio quam praedicationes centum.

Regulorum Africanorum mentionem libenter facit qui gentis quisque suae consensus declarandi periti fuerint. quorum in modum auctoritate sua maxima fretus utinam Afros suos in libertatem ita vindicet ut salutem praestet Europaeorum ibidem habitantium. Archiepiscopus est provinciae a promontorio Bonae Spei appellatae; quod forsitan mox in omen faustum convertatur. spem enim hic bonam praebet finem iam adesse laborum a gente sua tam diu perlatorum, gentes ibi diversas consiliis sagacissimis conciliatas pace salubri ac frugifera esse fructuras.

Praesento vobis φωνὴν ἀφώνων, Archiepiscopum Reverendissimum Desmondum Tutu, praemio Nobeliano ob pacem conservatam honestatum, Collegii Regii Londiniensis Socium, Cancellarium ipsum Universitatis Promontorii Occidentalis, ut admittatur honoris causa ad gradum Doctoris in Sacra Theologia.

MOST REVEREND DESMOND TUTU
Archbishop of Cape Town

AT last we have with us the man whom we have seen and heard so often on our television sets. Here is a Defender of our Faith and a Champion of Freedom, who has energetically defended the rights of all the peoples of South Africa. In honouring Archbishop Tutu there are others whom we must likewise honour: it befits us to praise that noble army of martyrs, who have in all places endured immense hardship for the sake of justice and peace.

Desmond Tutu has been aptly compared with the Old Testament prophets, for it is his wont to speak out frankly whatsoever things are true, even though they may seem obnoxious to government Ministers. His pronouncements are greatly needed. Everybody knows about the system of *apartheid,* concocted by former Ministers to separate black Africans from people of European origin. Our honorand has spent virtually all his life fighting this unspeakable system. Its very name is ill-omened and abominable, and I hesitate to pronounce it in this Theatre, dedicated to the humane arts and sciences. The system has been weakened, but not yet eliminated. Archbishop Tutu's objective is to destroy it without the destruction involved in war.

Although he read Theology at King's College London, and has spent a considerable time in England, he claims that his thinking is essentially African. He is steeped in the same broad love of humanity and has the same delight in talking and simplicity of mind which, he holds, are characteristic of Africans. There is not a trace of severity or pomp in him. Here without doubt is a 'mind touched by mortal things'. Recently when Nelson Mandela was freed (a release which we all realized was of great importance) we were privileged to witness the Archbishop himself 'treading the ground freely with his feet', and we could not forbear from remembering our Horace:

> My friend is back, it's good to revel.

That dance was more effective than a thousand sermons.

He likes to refer to traditional African chiefs who were skilled in enunciating the consensus of their people. It is our earnest hope that he will follow their example and make use of the great authority he has to achieve full freedom for his fellow Africans, while ensuring the safety of the Europeans who live with them in South Africa. He is Archbishop of the diocese called after the Cape of Good Hope. It may well be that this name will be a good omen. Desmond Tutu gives us grounds for hope that an end is at hand to the toils and troubles which his people has so long suffered and that the very different races in South Africa will be reconciled and enjoy the health and prosperity of peace.

I present the Voice of the Voiceless, the Most Reverend Desmond Tutu, Archbishop, winner of the Nobel Peace Prize, Fellow of King's College London, who is himself Chancellor of the University of the Western Cape, for the Honorary Degree of Doctor of Divinity.

1990

PRINCEPS CELSISSIMVS CAROLVS, PRINCEPS GVALLIAE

CANCELLARIVS MAGISTRI SCHOLARES
VNIVERSITATIS OXONIENSIS
OMNIBVS AD QVOS PRAESENTES
LITTERAE PERVENERINT
SALVTEM IN DOMINO SEMPITERNAM

CVM semper ex more nobis fuerit Regum Reginarumque nostrarum Filios honorare, praesertim qui negotia operosa libenter obeundo stirpe regali se dignissimos praestiterint:

CVMQVE Princeps Celsissimus CAROLVS, Princeps Gualliae, et in Caledonia et in terra sua Principali nec non apud Australenses educatus exemplum praebuerit varietatis gentium cum nobis consociatarum; Vniversitates autem Britannicas sit expertus, qui apud Cantabrigienses ad gradum laboris causa admissus sit; studiosus etiam fuerit pro iuventute totius regni universa, conciliis duobus regiis quae iuvenibus auxilium praebent salutare praefectus, quorum alterum Principale vocatum ipse fundavit:

NOS ERGO, cum caritatem professi Regiae Domus, cui plurimis nos vinculis coniungi gloriamur, tum Principi ipsi Coniugique et Filio bona optantes omnia atque augurantes, in frequenti Congregationis Domo praedictum Principem Doctorem in Iure Civili renuntiamus eumque vi ac virtute huius Diplomatis omnibus iuribus et privilegiis adficimus quae ad hunc gradum spectant.

IN CVIVS REI TESTIMONIVM sigillum Vniversitatis quo hac in parte utimur adponendum curavimus.

Datum in Domo nostra Congregationis die XVIII° mensis Maii A.S. MCMLXXXIII.

HIS ROYAL HIGHNESS THE PRINCE CHARLES, PRINCE OF WALES

WHEREAS we have ever been accustomed to show honour to the Sons of our Monarchs, especially those who have gladly undertaken onerous duties and have thereby proved themselves worthy indeed of their royal lineage:

AND WHEREAS His Royal Highness PRINCE CHARLES, PRINCE OF WALES, has by his education in Scotland, in his own Principality, and in Australia reflected the diversity of nations in the Commonwealth; and has himself experience of the Universities of Britain, having been awarded a degree in Cambridge University by virtue of his own work; and has moreover been active in helping youth in general throughout the Kingdom, in particular as President of The Royal Jubilee Trusts and as President of The Prince's Trust which he himself established:

NOW THEREFORE WE, avowing our affection for the Royal Family, and proud of the many links which unite us, and hoping especially and praying that every good fortune will attend Prince Charles and his Wife and their Son, do here in this full House of Congregation proclaim the aforesaid Prince a DOCTOR in our Faculty of Civil Law and by power and virtue of this Diploma do hereby invest him with all privileges and rights of that Degree.

IN WITNESS WHEREOF we have caused to be affixed to this instrument the Seal of the University thereunto pertaining.

Given in our House of Congregation on the eighth day of May in the Year of Salvation 1983.

NOTES: The legalistic form of these diplomas and also much of the Latin wording are traditional and of very considerable antiquity, as shown, for example, by that conferring the degree of MA upon Samuel Johnson in 1755 (printed in full by Boswell). In the ceremonial of conferment, modern practice is mainly based upon the procedure adopted on 15 June, 1814, when, in the presence of the Prince Regent, the degree of DCL by diploma was conferred upon the Emperor of Russia and the King of Prussia, both of whom, in virtue of the rights acquired, at once joined with the rest of Convocation in voting the same degree to the next recipient – the Duke of Wellington. Since under recent changes in the constitution of the University degrees are no longer conferred by Convocation, the time-honoured reference in the diploma to a 'full Convocation of Masters Regent and non-Regent' (*in frequenti Magistrorum Regentium et non Regentium Convocatione*) is no longer appropriate.